How to use this Lawpack Kit

This Kit can help executors obtain probate or confirmation, and so conveniently, efficiently and economically administer the estate of someone who has died. However, you should use this Kit properly in order to avoid future problems. Here are some pointers:

- Read this Manual carefully. If after thorough examination you decide that this Kit does not meet your requirements, take professional advice.
- This Kit refers to the main probate, confirmation and associated forms. These are available to download from the Lawpack website (see box below) or from HM Revenue & Customs in loose-leaf paper form by calling 0300 123 1072. When completing forms, follow any guidance provided. A good general rule is to complete every section, even if only by saying 'Not applicable' or 'None', unless the form requires you not to do so. This demonstrates that you have not overlooked any section.
- Always use a pen, or type, on legal documents. Don't use pencil.
- Don't cross out or erase anything you've written on your final forms.

DOWNLOADABLE FORMS AND DOCUMENTS:

- ✔ PA1P Probate Application — deceased left a Will
- ✔ PA1A Probate Application — deceased left no Will
- ✔ Form IHT205 Return of Estate Information
- ✔ Form IHT400 Full Inheritance Tax Return
- ✔ Forms PA1a, IHT400 Notes and IHT206 – guidance on completing PA1, IHT400 and IHT205, respectively
- ✔ Form C1 Confirmation
- ✔ Form C5 (SE) Information about Small Estates
- ✔ Form C5 Return of estate information
- ✔ Form C3 guidance on completing C1 and C5
- ✔ Completed examples of selected forms
- ✔ Executor letters
- ✔ Example estate accounts
- ✔ Example legacy receipt

To access your probate or confirmation documents, all you need to do is:

1. Enter **www.lawpack.co.uk/P237** in your browser's address bar,
2. Under the heading **Updates and Downloads** enter the code printed below into the registration box.

   REGISTRATION CODE: **P2371511054**

3. Click the **Activate!** button to access your downloads

Contents

LAWPACK®

Do-it-yourself Kit

Executor Guide

Guidance Manual

Important Facts about this Lawpack Kit

This Lawpack Kit contains the information, instructions and forms necessary for executors to obtain a grant of probate or grant of letters of administration in England and Wales, or confirmation in Scotland. It is not suitable for use in Northern Ireland. It is important that you read and follow the instructions in 'How to use this Lawpack Kit' on page 3.

The information it contains has been carefully compiled from reliable sources but its accuracy is not guaranteed, as laws and regulations may change or be subject to differing interpretations. This is particularly true for any figures given, which are liable to change.

Neither this nor any other publication can take the place of professional advice on important legal matters. This Lawpack Kit is sold with the understanding that the publisher, author and retailer are not engaged in rendering legal services. If legal advice or other expert assistance is required, the services of a competent professional should be sought.

As with any legal matter, common sense should determine whether you need the assistance of professional services rather than relying solely on the information and forms in this Lawpack Kit.

We strongly urge you to take professional advice if:

- you do not understand the instructions or are uncertain how to complete and use a form correctly;
- what you want to do is not precisely covered by the information provided;
- the deceased owned or had an interest in property abroad or had written a Will abroad.

EXCLUSION OF LIABILITY AND DISCLAIMER

Whilst every effort has been made to ensure that this Lawpack product provides accurate and expert guidance, it is impossible to predict all the circumstances in which it may be used. Accordingly, neither the publisher, authors, nor approving organisation that has assisted in the production of this Lawpack product and updated or refined it, or whose name is credited as having so assisted and updated or refined it, nor retailers, nor any other suppliers shall be liable to any person or entity with respect to any loss or damage caused or alleged to be caused as a result of the use of the information contained in or omitted from this Lawpack product.

Lawpack gives you a limited guarantee. If for any reason you are not happy with your purchase, you may return it to us with your receipt within 30 days of the date of purchase for a full refund. In no event shall our liability exceed the purchase price of this Kit. Use of this Lawpack Kit constitutes acceptance of these terms.

Notes:

- Since 2005, it has been possible for same-sex partners to register their relationships, so becoming 'registered civil partners'. For many purposes, and for most of the rules related to Wills and intestacy, registered civil partners are treated in the same way as spouses. Similarly, the term 'spouse' applies equally to those in a same sex marriage as they do a heterosexual marriage following the enactment of the Marriage (Same Sex Couples) Act 2013. Throughout this Manual, for 'spouse' read 'spouse or civil partner'.
- For convenience (and for no other reason) 'him', 'he' and 'his' have been used throughout and should be read to include the equivalent female pronouns.

What is an executor?

When someone is named the executor of a Will, he is being asked to take responsibility for administering the estate of the person who made the Will, called the testator, upon the testator's death.

Acting as an executor should not be undertaken lightly. Immediately following the death, the executors are expected to begin their administrative duties; long after other mourners' lives have returned to normal, the executors will still be administering the estate. This entails corresponding with other parties, keeping meticulous records, filling out forms and being answerable to creditors, beneficiaries and the intentions of the deceased, as recorded in the Will.

Don't be put off by the term 'estate'. This simply refers to all the property a person leaves behind, whether its value be hundreds or millions of pounds. One person's assets may include homes, yachts and a Swiss bank account, while another leaves a wedding ring, some changes of clothes and a shoe box full of costume jewellery. Both have left estates to be accounted for and distributed.

Executors' duties can be summed up as: taking an inventory of the deceased's possessions and debts, collecting the assets, paying the bills and distributing the legacies (whether specific items, cash sums or residue) following the testator's wishes as closely as possible.

Grant of probate or confirmation

Executors have the power to deal with the deceased's assets from the date of death, but not until they receive what is called in England, Wales a 'grant of probate', or in Scotland 'confirmation', can they prove their authority to those institutions and authorities that hold assets in the deceased's name. In England abd Wales, grants of probate are issued by the High Court through Probate Registries. In Scotland, confirmation is issued by the Commissary Department of the Sheriff Court in the area where the deceased had been domiciled at death.

More than one executor

If the Will appoints only one executor, or if only one person is able and willing to act, a grant of probate or confirmation can be issued to one person. In England and Wales, if the Will appoints more than four executors, only four of them will be allowed to apply for the grant of probate. The others may renounce their right to apply for probate; or they may decide not to apply for the time being but to reserve their right to apply in the future so that if, for example, one of the acting executors dies before the estate has been fully administered, the executor with power reserved may take his place.

In England and Wales, if only one of a number of executors is taking out the grant of probate, it is usual for the other executor(s) to sign what's called a 'power reserved' letter, even if it's not anticipated that he will want to apply at any stage. By reserving the right to apply in this way, a non-acting executor can step in if the acting executor becomes incapacitated before the administration of the estate is complete. Where a person named as an executor is certain that he does not wish to apply for a grant of probate and that he never will under any circumstances he can sign a formal renunciation. In England and Wales, the Probate Registry provides a form necessary to renounce or reserve the right to apply for probate.

In Scotland, there is no limit on the number of executors who may be appointed under a Will, but for practical reasons, it is probably not desirable to have more than four. Confirmation is always issued in favour of all surviving executors who have been nominated and who haven't predeceased the deceased or declined office. There is no Scottish equivalent to the English, Welsh and Northern Irish power reserved option and any executor named in the Will but not wishing to have confirmation issued in his favour, must sign a 'declinature' to be submitted to the Sheriff Court with the application for confirmation.

No matter how many executors are named, for practical purposes it's usually easier if one of the executors undertakes the administrative tasks on behalf of them all (he is referred to in this guide as the 'first applicant'). The executors should meet to discuss the practical side of carrying out their duties. Whatever is agreed should be put in writing and signed by them all. In fact, all official paperwork may need to be signed by all executors, even if they agree that one of them is the first applicant (the exception being that in Scotland the application for confirmation [Form C1] needs to be signed by only one executor, but must beforehand be approved by all executors).

Caution: If it looks as though the deceased's estate is insolvent, i.e. the debts of the deceased and other liabilities of the estate, including funeral expenses, will exceed the value of the assets in the estate, executors should think carefully before applying for the grant of probate or confirmation and should seek professional legal advice.

Other personal representatives

If an executor renounces the right to take out the grant of probate or in Scotland if a nominated executor declines to accept office, any substitute executor named in the Will steps in and proceeds to apply for the grant of probate or confirmation. If no executor is named in the Will or if the executor named cannot or does not wish to act and no substitute is named, beneficiaries can apply to act as the deceased's personal representatives. A beneficiary acting as the testator's personal representative is, in England and Wales, known as the 'administrator' and the grant itself is called a 'grant of letters of administration with Will annexed'.

An administrator's duties are essentially the same as those of an executor. This guide refers to executors, but the rights and responsibilities of both are the same in most respects, whether the person doing the work is an executor or an administrator.

In England and Wales, beneficiaries may apply for a grant as the deceased's administrators in the following order of priority:

1. Any residuary beneficiary.
2. Any personal representative of a residuary beneficiary.
3. Any other 'legatee' (i.e. someone who receives a legacy).

4. Any personal representative of any other legatee.
5. Any creditor.

In Scotland, an executor appointed by a Will is called an 'executor-nominate' and an executor appointed by the Court is called an 'executor-dative' (appropriate where there is no Will, meaning the deceased died 'intestate' or where there is a Will but that it is not fully valid thus creating a 'partial intestacy'). Where there is a Will, but no executor has been named, or there is no surviving executor who agrees to accept office, the nearest relative would apply to the Court, and the position would be explained in the application.

If the conditions to obtain a nominate appointment cannot be met, it will be necessary to submit a petition to the Court for the appointment of an executor-dative. The order of priority to be appointed executor-dative follows the order of entitlement to succession to the intestate estate, (see flowchart on page 28).

In England and Wales, a minor (someone under the age of 18) cannot act as an executor. If a minor is the only executor appointed in a Will, his parents or guardian are entitled to take out a grant of letters of administration with Will annexed on his behalf. The minor has the right to apply for the grant of probate on reaching his 18th birthday, if the administration of the estate has not been completed.

In Scotland, a person reaching the age of 16 has legal capacity and in principle may act as executor; however, there can be practical difficulties and it is not recommended that a person below the age of 18 be appointed executor. Where a child below the age of 16 has been named as executor and has parents or a guardian, the parents/guardian may seek appointment and be confirmed as executor on behalf of the child, or may decline office on the child's behalf.

If the deceased left no Will and died intestate, the estate is distributed according to the rules of intestacy. In England, and Wales, the executors are again known as administrators and the grant is called a 'grant of letters of administration'. In Scotland, the individuals are, when appointed, known as executors-dative but the grant is still known as confirmation. In England and Wales, when there is no Will, administrators are appointed in the following order of priority:

1. The deceased's spouse.
2. Any child of the deceased and any issue of a child who died before the deceased.
3. The parents of the deceased.
4. Brothers and sisters of the whole blood of the deceased and the issue of any who died before the deceased.
5. Brothers and sisters of the half blood of the deceased and the issue of any who died before the deceased.
6. Grandparents of the deceased.
7. Uncles and aunts of the whole blood and the issue of any who died before the deceased.
8. Uncles and aunts of the half blood and the issue of any who died before the deceased.

In England and Wales, the maximum number of administrators is four, whether there is a Will or the person died intestate. A sole administrator may take out the grant only where none of the beneficiaries is under 18 or where no life interest arises. If either of these is the case, the grant must be issued to a minimum of two administrators.

Intestacy in England and Wales is discussed later in this guide.

In Scotland, contemporary Sheriff Court practice is that the person or persons entitled to receive the deceased's estate under the rules of intestate succession (which post-date the creation of the above order of preference) will be deemed entitled to the office of executor-dative. The same legislation provides that the surviving spouse has the right – treated in practice as the exclusive right, but in practice a complicated area – to the office of executor-dative, where he is entitled to the whole of the intestate estate under the succession rules. In Scotland, in an intestate estate no 'liferent' (or life interest) arises – the Scottish rules of intestate succession are explained, beginning on page 26.

Should a professional adviser be instructed?

Executors can seek professional advice from either a bank if it offers this service, trust corporation or solicitor, or from a stockbroker or other adviser with a view to performing specific duties even if they do not use a professional to submit the probate or confirmation application. Whether an executor handles all the tasks involved in administering the estate or uses professional advisers is a matter of choice and convenience. Any fees properly incurred are paid out of the estate, subject to the terms of the Will.

This Kit is designed to help the layperson sort out a simple, straightforward Will or intestacy. If the Will or the estate is complex, a solicitor should be consulted. If you are in any doubt, seek professional advice. Some signs that a solicitor should be involved include the following:

1. The estate is insolvent.
2. A beneficiary cannot be contacted.
3. Someone intends to challenge the Will.
4. There is some question of the Will's validity, or the Will cannot be found.
5. Someone stands to inherit a life interest in (or in Scotland a 'liferent' of) the estate.
6. Beneficiaries include children under the age of 18 (in Scotland, 16) and a trust is set up for them.
7. The deceased owned a business or was a partner in a business or owned agricultural property.
8. The deceased was a Name (i.e. an investor) in Lloyd's of London insurance market.
9. A trust is set up under the Will.
10. Any house or land in the estate has an unregistered title.
11. The Inheritance Tax calculations are particularly complex.
12. One or more beneficiaries wish to vary the terms of the Will in so far as it affects their entitlement.
13. There is no Will but a cohabitee neither married to, nor in

a civil partnership with the deceased, may wish to make a claim on the intestate estate.

14. Heritable property in Scotland, where there is no survivorship destination in the title.

When death occurs

When someone dies, a doctor should be called. He will issue a medical certificate stating the cause or causes of death, along with a notice setting out who is eligible to register the death with the local Registrar of Births and Deaths.

Registering the death

In England and Wales, if the death has occurred inside a house or public building, the following people may act as informant, in the following order:

1. A relative of the deceased who was present at the death.
2. A relative of the deceased who was present during the final stages of the illness.
3. A relative of the deceased who lives in the district where the death occurred.
4. Anyone who was present at the death.
5. Someone in authority in the building where the death occurred who was aware of the circumstances of the death; for example, the owner of a nursing home or the warden of sheltered accommodation.
6. Any resident of the building where the death occurred, if he was aware of the circumstances of the death.
7. The person who accepts responsibility for arranging the funeral.

If the death occurred outside a house or public building, the following people are eligible to register the death in the following order:

1. A relative of the deceased able to provide the Registrar with the necessary details.
2. Anyone who was present at the death.
3. The person who found the body.
4. The person in charge of the body (the police if the body is unidentified).
5. The person who accepts responsibility for arranging the funeral.

In Scotland, the death must be registered by:

1. Any relative of the deceased.
2. Any person present at the death.
3. The executor or other legal representative of the deceased.
4. The occupier at the time of death of the premises where the death occurred.
5. Any other person having knowledge of the particulars to be registered, if there is no person as above.

In England and Wales, within five days of the death the informant must take the medical certificate to the Registrar of Deaths, or must send written notice. (In Scotland, post-Covid, the Registrar will now phone the person who is registering the death to obtain the details.) You can generally book an appointment to register the death at a local Register Office online or by telephone. In England and Wales, the deceased's medical card should be given to the Registrar as well, if it has not already been sent by the doctor direct to the Register Office. Sometimes this is done electronically by the doctor.The Registrar will ask for other details about the deceased:

1. The date and place of death (birth certificate should be produced if available).
2. The full name of the deceased, including any maiden name.
3. The date and place of birth of the deceased.
4. The occupation of the deceased.
5. The name, date of birth and occupation of the deceased's spouse (and in Scotland, former spouses), whether or not still living.
6. The deceased's usual address.
7. Whether the deceased received any state pension, other pension or allowance.
8. The date of birth of any surviving spouse.
9. In Scotland, the full names and occupations of the parents of the deceased should also be provided (if known).

The death certificate

Once the death has been registered, the informant will be given a death certificate, which is a copy of the register entry. In Scotland, he will also be given a certificate for the funeral director dealing with the funeral, a free abbreviated death certificate, and a Tell Us Once Service (see below) notification of death form to assist in obtaining or adjusting benefits. There is a small charge for each copy of the full death certificate, and it's sensible to get three or four copies. The executors may need to send copies to the deceased's bank, to the registrars of companies in which he held shares, to insurance companies holding policies written in trust and, in England and Wales, to the Probate Registry. Although you can have the certificate returned to you once it has been inspected, it may be more convenient to circulate several copies at once.

Note: A while after the death, the cost of a copy of the death certificate may increase. The period varies depending on the register office, so it's worth checking if it's probable further copies will be needed.

Tell Us Once service

When you register the death, the registrar may ask you if you would like to use the Tell Us Once service. This is a government service which lets you inform most government organisations of the death of the deceased in one go. Using this service can save you time and speed up your dealings with various government departments such as the Department of Work and Pensions (who would deal with benefits and the State Pension that the deceased might have received). If the registrar does not complete the Tell Us Once service with you, make sure that you obtain a unique reference number from them so that you can complete the service yourself either online or on the phone. They will provide the relevant contact details for you.

The Will

If the executors are prepared for their duties, they may have been in possession of a copy of the Will even before the death and know the location of the original. They may know of the deceased's instructions concerning organ donation, disposal of the body, and funeral wishes. All of this information is needed in the first hours following death.

Arranging the funeral is not specifically the duty of executors and should be handled by whoever is most aware of the deceased's wishes. The Will, however, may include funeral instructions and/or the deceased's wishes. Anyone who manages the funeral is entitled to have the account settled out of money from the estate.

If there is no opportunity for preparation before the death, the Will must be located to determine who has been named its executor(s). If no Will is found at the deceased's home, it may have been sent to his bank or solicitor for safekeeping or to Lawpack's Will Storage Service. In England and Wales, it may have been deposited at the Principal Registry (formerly Somerset House), in which case a deposit certificate will have been issued on receipt of the Will; the Will can be reclaimed by sending the certificate to:

Newcastle District Probate Registry
2nd Floor Kings Court
Earl Grey Way
North Shields
NE29 6AR

safecustodywillsenquiries@justice.gov.uk
Tel 0300 303 0648

If a Will is found, ascertain that it is the deceased's last Will by making enquiries at, for example, the deceased's bank and solicitor. It must bear the signature of the deceased (in Scotland, it must be signed on every page) and of an appropriate witnesses (or single witness in Scotland). For Scottish Wills, made pre-1995, it would be best to seek professional advice, because the signing position was different and there were different types of Will.

In England and Wales, probate may be granted on a copy, but you should notify the Probate Registry as soon as possible that the original cannot be found. The Registry will tell you what evidence is needed as proof that the original Will had not been revoked by being destroyed before death.

In Scotland, the Principal Will is required if only a copy of the signed Will can be found. It may possible for the executors to treat the estate as 'testate' and proceed to wind up the estate in accordance with the copy Will but it will be necessary in the first instance to raise an action in the Court of Session in Edinburgh to 'prove the tenor' of the original signed Will using the copy and professional advice should be sought. If this fails, the estate must be treated as intestate and wound up accordingly.

The necessity of a formal reading of the Will before hopeful beneficiaries, or a solicitor, is a myth. There is no legal requirement for any reading but it is courteous to write to beneficiaries to inform them of their entitlement under the Will.

There may be some doubt as to who the beneficiaries are under the Will. Many Wills describe certain beneficiaries in terms of groups of people, for example 'my children,' rather than naming them. The expression 'my children' includes, by law, children conceived at the time of the deceased's death and subsequently born alive, adopted children and illegitimate children. In some circumstances, stepchildren are also included.

In England and Wales, if the Will was executed after 3 April 1988, children whose parents were married to each other at the time of their birth are treated in the same way as those whose parents were not, even if the executors have no knowledge of the children's existence. If the Will was executed before then, the executors will not be liable to a testator's child born outside marriage if they didn't know of his existence. These rules apply unless it is clear from the Will that the deceased intended otherwise.

In Scotland, if the Will was executed on or after 25 November 1968, in determining who should be the beneficiaries of an estate, no distinction is to be drawn between legitimate and illegitimate relationships. This applies to all relationships including the construction of such terms as grandchildren, brother, cousin, etc. These rules apply unless it is clear from the Will that the deceased intended otherwise.

For Wills executed in Scotland prior to that date, the common law continues to apply and expressions such as 'children' or 'issue' (another term for children) are presumed to refer to legitimate relationships only, unless the Will indicates otherwise. Providing the executor is acting in good faith having made all reasonable enquiries, statute gives the executor some protection, allowing him to distribute the estate without instigating an exhaustive search for potential illegitimate claimants or any person adopted by the deceased who would also have a claim on the estate. If there is any doubt about this, it would be best to seek legal advice.

Generally, if a beneficiary named in a Will has died before the testator, the gift to him will simply not take effect. However, if that beneficiary is a child, grandchild or great-grandchild or remoter issue of the testator (or in Scotland, a nephew or niece of the testator, but the extension of the principle is limited to those specific relatives only), and he has left children of his own, the children step into or may step into their parent's shoes and their entitlement under the Will, shared equally between them.

In England and Wales (but not in Scotland), if the deceased married after making the Will and the Will was not expressed to be in expectation of the marriage, the Will is automatically revoked. Divorce by the testator, however, does not revoke a Will, but in England and Wales (but not in Scotland), the former spouse is treated as if he died on the date of the divorce so that, unless a contrary intention appears from the Will, he cannot take a gift under the Will or act as an executor.

In England and Wales (but not in Scotland), if the deceased married after making the Will and the Will was not expressed to be in expectation of the marriage, the Will is automatically revoked. Divorce, however, does not revoke a Will, but in

England and Wales (but not in Scotland), the former spouse is treated as if he died on the date of the divorce so that the any gift to the former spouse under the Will does not take effect and they cannot act as an executor.

It is important to note that in Scotland so called 'legal rights' of the spouse and issue of the deceased can affect the division of an estate, regardless of the terms of a valid Will – see page 27 for an explanation of legal rights. Executors must deal with this issue as part of the administration of a testate estate.

If the executors are uncertain as to the interpretation of other parts of the Will, they should seek the advice of a solicitor to avoid the risk of distributing the money wrongly.

Once probate or confirmation is granted the Will becomes a public document, but until then the beneficiaries may know nothing of their legacies, unless the deceased told them before he died. However, the executors will usually tell the beneficiaries that they have been left a legacy, although it's impossible to be specific about the amount if it's a legacy of residue or part of residue. But no legacy can be guaranteed at this stage as the Will may be found invalid, may be challenged, or the assets of the estate may not be sufficient to pay all the legacies.

Duties of an executor

In preparation for dealing with the assets and liabilities of the estate, some administrative tasks should be attended to by the executors as soon as possible.

Have a mail redirect implemented from the deceased's postal address to that of the first applicant, the executor who is to handle day-to-day business and personal affairs. If the home is to be left unoccupied, the executors should ensure that it's securely locked; that water, electricity and gas supplies have been turned off and mail redirected.

The executors should also ensure that there are both current buildings and contents insurance policies on the home. The executors may be held liable by any beneficiary who receives less from the estate than he should have because of a burglary, fire or other loss. The insurers should be notified of the death, advised that the property is unoccupied, and be given the names and addresses of the executors. If there are particularly valuable items at the deceased's home and it's to be left unoccupied, it may be better to remove them for safekeeping.

Finally, the executors should open an executors' bank account into which they will eventually deposit the proceeds of assets and from which they will pay the bills of the deceased.

Make a thorough search of the deceased's papers and online records for the documents that will be needed to finalise the deceased's affairs. These will include, but not be limited to:

- Cheque books
- Bank statements
- Savings certificates and other National Savings assets
- Outstanding bills
- Share certificates and stockbroker's details
- Car registration documents
- Mortgage papers
- Insurance and pension documentation
- Information on jewellery and collectables; for example, insurance valuations
- Title deeds
- Tax assessments, returns, and other tax papers
- Any other assets or debts that are located

The executors' aims are to:

1. Identify the assets of the estate and assess their value at date of death.
2. Identify the deceased's debts and pay them.
3. Distribute the legacies.

Is a grant of probate or confirmation necessary?

Whilst itemising the assets of the estate, the executors must bear in mind that it may not be necessary to apply for a grant of probate (England and Wales) or for confirmation (Scotland). Whether or not a grant is required depends not only on the size of the deceased's estate, but also on the kinds of assets in it. Normally, a grant is required where the value of the deceased's estate (after paying the funeral account) exceeds £5,000. The grant vests authority in the executors to deal with the estate. Without that authority, the executors would be relying solely on the validity of the Will. (In Scotland, where there is heritable property, with no survivorship destination in the title, confirmation will be required. If there is no heritable property, it will depend on the value of the whole estate.) If the deceased only left a great deal of cash, personal items having a high market value and a very expensive car, there is no need to apply for a grant of probate or confirmation because executors need no formal proof of their authority to gather in and distribute such assets. On the other hand, if the deceased had a bank account and shares with a net value of over £5,000, or if the deceased's home needs to be sold or transferred to a beneficiary, a grant will be necessary so the executors can obtain formal authority to gather in and deal with these assets.

Certain authorities can pay sums due on death to the person entitled under a Will or intestacy without requiring sight of a grant of probate, as long as the amount payable is (normally) less than £5,000. The assets concerned include:

- **National Savings, including prizes won on Premium Bonds.** In order to claim, the executors need to complete Form NSA 904, which is available from post offices, and send it to the address given on that form for the type of account held, together with a registrar's copy of the death certificate.
- **Building society accounts, deposits with friendly societies, trade union deposits of members, arrears of salary or pension due to government or local government employees and police and firemen's pensions.** The executors should write to the relevant authority, asking for a claim form and sending a registrar's copy of the death certificate.

Other assets that may be realised without the executors needing to produce the grant of probate or confirmation are:

- **Nominated property.** Until 1981, the holder of certain National Savings investments and government stock could nominate someone to receive them on his death. After 1981, no new nominations could be made, but those made before that year are valid. Such a nomination takes effect independently of the deceased's Will or intestacy and independently of any grant of probate. The person nominated can have such stocks transferred into his name or redeemed on producing the death certificate. There is no upper limit on the value of the nominated property which can be dealt with in this way, but if the institution is concerned that the estate may be large enough for Inheritance Tax (IHT) to be paid on it, it may require the executors to obtain a certificate from HM Revenue & Customs (HMRC) to show that any such tax has been paid.
- **Jointly held assets.** When two people hold property jointly (as 'joint tenants' in England and Wales, or in Scotland where there is a 'survivorship destination'), on the death of one of them, his share of the asset passes directly to the other by right of survivorship, regardless of the provisions of the Will or the intestacy rules. Such assets might include a house or flat, or bank or building society accounts. No grant of probate or confirmation is required to transfer the deceased's share of these assets to the surviving joint holder.

  If the property is a house or flat in England or Wales that is registered land, a registrar's copy of the death certificate should be sent to the Land Registry (www.gov.uk) to enable the survivor to be registered as the sole surviving owner of the property. If the property is unregistered, a registrar's copy of the death certificate should be kept with the title deeds which would need to be produced if the property is sold.

  In Scotland, with property where there is a survivorship destination, no action is required (whether or not the property is registered in the Land Register of Scotland or the General Register of Sasines, www.ros.gov.uk) except that a copy of the death certificate should be held as part of the surviving owner's title. If the joint asset is a bank or building society account, a registrar's copy of the death certificate should be sent to the relevant bank or building society so the deceased's name may be removed from the account. Therefore, if the deceased's estate consists solely of jointly held assets, there would normally be no need for the executors to apply for a grant of probate or confirmation.

  However, in Scotland, where one person opens a bank or building society account in joint names, unless it is specified at the outset that they are actually making a gift to the joint account holder, the fact that there is a joint account holder is significant only for the bank's administrative purposes. The bank may well automatically transfer the account after death to the joint account holder, but this does not mean that the joint holder is necessarily entitled to the whole account. The entitlement to the account (and therefore the proportion attributable to the deceased) will depend upon the proportions in which each account holder contributed to and made withdrawals from the account. It may ultimately be necessary to recover some funds from the joint account holder to meet claims on the deceased's estate and satisfy bequests in the Will.

Probate Registries

In England & Wales, once it has been ascertained that a grant is required, the executors will need to obtain the probate application forms, available to downloadd with this Kit. Registries used to ask applicants to visit their offices to swear an oath but this is no longer required. Instead the application forms contain a statement of truth which must be signed by the applicants. It is now also possible to apply for a grant of representation online using the HM Courts and Tribunals Service portal which can be accessed via the government website: https://rb.gy/9sf75g.

In Scotland, the Sheriff Court issues confirmation to the executors or their legal agents.

Financial records

During the administration of the estate, the executors must keep track of every financial transaction, no matter how small. The money and assets belonging to the estate must be kept entirely separate from the executors' personal money and assets. Out-of-pocket expenses of the executors should be recorded as carefully as the payment of bank charges, probate or confirmation fees, or Inheritance Taxes.

Although executors are paid for their efforts only if the Will so specifies, expenses the executors incur, such as postage, travel costs, telephone bills, etc., can be paid from the estate.

More importantly, the executors must be able to account for every penny of the testator's estate. They have a fiduciary responsibility (i.e. one of trust) to the creditors and beneficiaries of the estate. When the estate has been fully administered, the executors will need to draw up accounts to demonstrate to the beneficiaries how the assets of the estate were spent or distributed.

Paying Inheritance Tax

Once a thorough valuation of the deceased's assets and liabilities is completed, any Inheritance Tax due must be paid before applying for the grant of probate or confirmation. However, few financial institutions will hand over the funds of the deceased until there is a grant of probate or confirmation to prove the executors' authority.

If the deceased had funds in a National Savings account or held National Savings Certificates and Premium Bonds, National Savings may remit funds direct to HMRC to cover all or part of the tax, thereby permitting the grant of probate or confirmation. Similar arrangements may be made between a building society account and HMRC. Other banks may be willing to arrange a loan to the executors in order to pay the Inheritance Tax.

As an alternative to the above, it may be possible to arrange for the tax to be paid direct from the account in the deceased's sole name in a bank or building society, using HMRC Form IHT423. You will need to obtain a tax reference from HMRC for the estate. When you are ready to apply for probate, send the Form IHT423 to the bank or building society and they will pay HMRC direct from the account.

If for cash flow reasons, you are paying the IHT from your personal funds you can pay this online through the gov.uk website.

Identifying beneficiaries

Once the liabilities of the estate have been paid, the executors identify the beneficiaries of the estate: either those named in the Will or those entitled under the intestacy rules. If the executors distribute the estate incorrectly, they are personally liable to the rightful beneficiaries and to creditors about whom they know or should have known. In Scotland, executors are personally liable for six months after death.

In England and Wales, to protect themselves from unknown creditors and beneficiaries, the executors can follow a statutory procedure which involves the placing of advertisements for creditors in the *London Gazette* for England and Wales at:

London Gazette
PO Box 35
Norwich
NR7 7WD
www.thegazette.co.uk
E: london@thegazette.co.uk
T: 0870 600 33 22

Executors must also advertise in a newspaper circulating in the area where the deceased lived and, particularly if he owned a business, the area where he worked at the time of death. If land is to be distributed, an advertisement should also be placed in a newspaper circulating in the district where the land is situated. The advertisements should state that anyone with a claim against or an interest in the estate must make their claim known within a stated time (not less than two months) from the date of the notice, after which the executors may distribute the estate, having regard only to those claims of which they have notice. After the stated time, in England and Wales, anyone who has not come forward cannot make a claim against the executors, although they may claim against the beneficiaries of the estate into whose hands assets have passed.

Advertising for unknown creditors may not be necessary if there is no reason to suspect that the deceased has incurred debts other than those known to the executor. In Scotland, there is no statutory requirement to advertise for creditors, but the executors may consider this prudent, depending upon the level of information in relation to the deceased and his personal circumstances.

Note: Unlike an executor, an administrator in England and Wales can place statutory advertisements only after the grant of letters of administration has been issued.

Taking stock

As a first step, the executors should list those assets which they know, based on personal observation or findings, the deceased owned. This guide includes a checklist below which sets out the most commonly owned assets.

Following this inventory by observation, the executor sends notification of the death to the deceased's bank, building society, accountant, insurance company and other institutions. The letters to the bank and building society should request information about each account and instruct them to stop all unpaid cheques and standing orders. Also ask for a list of deeds and other documents held on behalf of the deceased; for example, life policies, as at the date of death.

Executors don't have to wait to receive the grant of probate or confirmation to begin this notification and inventory, but a copy must be sent to each institution when it's received from the Probate Registry in England and Wales or the Commissary Department of the Sheriff Court concerned in Scotland. For the initial correspondence, it's sufficient to enclose a copy of the death certificate.

The goal is to get in writing the value of all the assets and debts as at the time of death. This information must be provided on the probate or confirmation forms. Even if an asset is left as a legacy to a beneficiary, it must be listed and accounted for in the inventory. Similarly, you must obtain the value of the deceased's share of any jointly held assets including those passing by survivorship.

Valuing debts

The following is a checklist of debts the deceased might owe. Information on any of these liabilities that apply should be included on page 8 of HMRC Form IHT400 and Schedule IHT419. They are also included on the Form C1 for Scottish estates. This is the return of the testator's whole estate for Inheritance Tax purposes, discussed further on page 18. If necessary, it's generally possible to request a delay in payment of debts until the grant has been obtained and funds are available.

Debt	Action
1. Water rates **2.** Telecoms bill **3.** Subscription TV bill	Ask for a bill to the date of death.
4. Electricity bill **5.** Gas bill	Take a meter reading on the date of death, or as soon afterwards as possible and ask for a bill to that date.
6. Loan or overdraft	Write to the bank for the outstanding balance.
7. Credit card bills	Write to the credit card company asking for the amount of any outstanding balance.
8. Mail-order catalogue bill	Write to notify the company on the death and to ask whether any outstanding balance is due.

9. Rent arrears
10. Hire purchase payments
11. Debts owed by the deceased to other individuals
12. Council Tax
13. Outstanding Income Tax and Capital Gains Tax
14. Mortgage
15. In Scotland, 'legal rights' are automatically payable after ordinary debts, in both testate and intestate estates; see page 29 for further details.

Reasonable funeral expenses are also counted as a liability of the estate, including the cost of a gravestone. If the person arranging the funeral is in receipt of Income Support, Tax Credits or Housing Benefit, he may be able to apply for a Funeral Expenses Payment from the government for a payment to cover reasonable funeral expenses. However, the cost is repaid out of the estate if money subsequently becomes available. More details can be found online at https://www.gov.uk/funeral-payments.

Asset checklist

To help the executors make an inventory of assets, the following checklist itemises some of the typical ones found in an estate. As you go through it, refer to the probate forms which must be filed in England and Wales with the Probate Registry, or in Scotland with the Commissary Department of the Sheriff Court concerned. Not all the assets listed here are specifically categorised on Form IHT400; those not listed should be recorded on pages 15 and 16 of Form IHT400 and their total value included in Box 76 on page 7 of Form IHT400. In Scotland, the application to the Sheriff Court for confirmation (Form C1) includes a full inventory of the deceased's assets and their values. This form can be referred to for its terms where appropriate when completing Form IHT400, thus avoiding the necessity of duplicating the information already contained in Form C1.

House or flat

If the deceased owned his own home jointly with another person, only the deceased's share of the home is treated as part of his estate. It will usually be a half-share unless the owners held the property as tenants in common or in some other specific proportions and the title deeds specify that they hold it in unequal shares. If two or more joint owners hold a property in England and Wales as tenants in common, or in Scotland without a survivorship destination, each person can leave his own share of the property to whoever he wishes under his Will. However, if they hold the property in England and Wales as joint tenants or in Scotland where there is a survivorship destination, the share of a person who dies automatically passes to the survivor or survivors.

If the precise value is not relevant for calculating Inheritance Tax due on the estate (e.g. because the property or the deceased's share of it is to go to the deceased's spouse, or in Scotland if there is no requirement to calculate the value of the spouse's 'prior rights' on intestacy – see page 27), an approximate value will normally be acceptable. The executor should, however, ascertain as accurate an estimate of value as is reasonably practicable. He may estimate the value himself by reference to the prices which similar properties in the area are fetching, or ask an estate agent for an informal valuation.

In some circumstances, it's better to ask an estate agent or surveyor to make a formal valuation, for which a fee may be charged. For instance, if the property is to be transferred to a beneficiary as part of a legacy instead of cash, (or in Scotland as part of a claim for prior rights) then the executor should have a formal valuation to ensure that the distribution among the beneficiaries is fair.

Whichever method is used, in an estate which is likely to be taxable, the value given will be checked by the District Valuer for HMRC who may challenge it if it appears to be too low. If the property is sold soon after the death (although the executors will not be able to complete the sale until they have the grant showing their entitlement to deal with the property), the District Valuer would normally seek to substitute the sale price for the value submitted in the probate or confirmation application. Details of the property should be included in Schedule IHT405, Houses, land, buildings and interests in land.

If there is a mortgage on the deceased's house or flat, the mortgage lender should be notified. You should give the deceased's name, address and mortgage account number and enclose a copy of the death certificate. You will need to know how much of the mortgage was outstanding at the date of death, and whether there is a life assurance or mortgage protection policy linked to the mortgage. If there is, you should ask whether the cover is sufficient to repay the mortgage and whether there will be any surplus remaining after repayment.

Bank account

The executors must write to the deceased's banks and, if there are also building society accounts, to the building societies, with a registrar's copy of the death certificate, to inform them of the death and to instruct them to stop all unpaid cheques, direct debits and standing orders.You should also ask for a list of all deeds, share certificates and other documents held on the deceased's behalf and the balances on the deceased's accounts (including joint accounts) at the date of death, with a separate figure for interest which had been earned on the money to that date, but not credited to the account. This information is needed for Form IHT400. It's also useful to ask, in the same letter, what interest has been credited to the deceased's account during the tax year in which he died and whether it was paid net of tax or gross. This information will be needed for the tax return for the year to the date of death. The executors may also request statements detailing transactions in the seven years before the date of death in order to help establish whether the deceased made lifetime gifts which are relevant for calculating the IHT due.

The executors will also need to open a bank account in their own names to enable them to pay in the proceeds of sales of assets of the estate, and to write cheques or otherwise use funds to discharge liabilities. The executors' full names and addresses should be given to the bank, which will send a mandate for completion and signature by the executors.

Any cheques which are made payable to the deceased but which were not paid into his account before the death may be able to be paid into his account or the executors' account, but the bank may insist that such cheques be endorsed in favour of the executors. Once a copy of the grant of probate or confirmation has been shown to the bank, the bank can transfer the balance on the deceased's account to the executors' account.

Stocks and shares

If the deceased owned any shares, the certificates may be at the deceased's home or with his bank, solicitor or stockbroker. If they are at the home and it's to be left unoccupied, it's best to remove them for safe keeping. It may be desirable to check with the registrar of each of the companies in which the shares were held to make sure that the holdings evidenced by the certificates are correct. The name and address of the registrar can usually be found on the counterfoil of the share certificate or you can look them up in the *Register of Registrars*, a publication which can be found in most reference libraries.

Sometimes, shareholdings are in the nominee name of the shareholder's stockbroker and the stockbroker will have the share certificates. If that is the case, there is no need to write to each of the company registrars, but the stockbroker should be notified of the death and sent a copy of the death certificate.

If any share certificates cannot be found, the executors may need to sign a statutory declaration and indemnity before selling them or transferring them to a beneficiary, for which the registrar of the company will charge a fee. It states that the executors have searched for the certificate and believe it to be lost, and the executors indemnify the company against any loss if the certificate comes to light later in the hands of a person who has a better claim to ownership of the shares than the executors do. Some shareholdings may be uncertificated and therefore no certificates are involved.

Once a complete list of shareholdings has been compiled, the executors can ask a stockbroker for a probate or confirmation valuation, for which he will charge a fee, generally a fixed sum per holding. Alternatively, executors may make their own valuation by referring to the Stock Exchange Daily Official List (SEDOL) for the day the deceased died. The List is available at public libraries or can be bought from the Publications Section of the Stock Exchange in London – see www.londonstockexchange.com.

For probate or confirmation purposes, the value of a stock is the lower of the two values quoted, plus a quarter of the difference between those values; for example, for a share quoted at 96–98p for that day, 96.5p would be the probate or confirmation value.

If any of the shares are quoted Ex-Dividend (or 'XD'), there is a dividend due to the deceased that has not yet been paid. If you are obtaining a valuation from a broker, he will include such dividends in the valuation. Otherwise, telephone the registrar of the company who will be able to give the value of the dividend, or alternatively search on the company's website in the shareholder information section. The dividend per share may be a gross figure; in which case multiply it by the number of shares held by the deceased. If the deceased died before 6 April 2016 you will also need to deduct tax at ten per cent to arrive at the net figure which will appear on the dividend cheque. The notional 10 per cent tax credit was abolished from 6 April 2016.

The value of unit trust units can be obtained from the fund manager of the relevant unit trust company. If the deceased owned shares in any unquoted companies, write to the company secretary of each one asking for a valuation of the shares at the date of death.

A list of all shares and their values should be included on Schedules IHT411 and IHT412. Dividends (the net figure) are listed separately; any dividends which were uncashed at the time of death should also be included. The total values are then included in Boxes 62 – 67 on page 7 of Form IHT400. If the deceased had a personal equity plan (PEP) or an Individual Savings Account (ISA), its provider can give a valuation as at the date of death.

Businesses

If the deceased had an interest in a business, it will need to be valued by the business' accountant, backed up by a copy of the latest three years' accounts and a copy of any partnership agreement, as requested in Schedule IHT413 of Form IHT400.

Car

A local garage can provide an accurate valuation of the deceased's car. On the other hand, the executors may prefer simply to sell the car at arm's length on the open market soon after the death and use the sale price as the value at the date of death. For antique or classic cars, a professional valuation should be obtained.

Jewellery

An overall valuation will usually be acceptable for jewellery, although if an individual piece is worth more than £1,500 it should be valued separately. Similarly, a formal valuation would be prudent in Scotland if the estate is intestate and there are prior and legal rights to be calculated (see page 27). A jeweller can give a valuation, for which he will usually charge a fee. You should tell the jeweller that the valuation is needed for probate or confirmation purposes to ensure you receive an estimate of the price for which he could sell the item, not the replacement value, which may be much higher.

Works of art

One way of finding out whether a particular painting or sculpture is of value is to see if it's separately listed on the deceased's home contents insurance policy, but that is by no means necessarily foolproof. An art dealer can give a valuation of any works of art. Make it clear that you are asking for the price it would fetch at auction at the date of death, not the value for which it should be insured.

Other possessions

There is no need to compile a detailed list of all of the deceased's possessions, such as furniture and personal effects. However, if the estate is Scottish and intestate, an auctioneer's formal inventory and valuation of personal effects and household contents will assist the calculation of beneficiaries' entitlements and would be wise. Otherwise, the executor's reasonable and fair estimate of their total value can be given, based on what they might fetch if sold second-hand or, if appropriate, at auction at the date of death. Separate details, and preferably formal valuations of individual items worth over £500 should be given, as should the values of items such as vehicles, boats and aircraft, antiques, works of art or collections. This information should be included in Schedule IHT407 of the Form IHT400. HMRC can challenge asset values if they appear particularly low. In the case of a husband and wife, household possessions are generally treated as being held jointly between them, and so their total value should be divided by two to give the value of the deceased's share. Of course, if the deceased owned something outright, the entire value of the item is considered part of the deceased's estate for Inheritance Tax purposes.

National Savings

There is a special procedure for National Savings accounts. The executor must complete Form NS&I 904 and send it to the address given on the form for that type of account. For National Savings certificates, the executor will need to write to National Savings asking for a letter confirming the value of the certificates held by the deceased at the date of death. In England and Wales, the Probate Registry will need to see this letter. In Scotland, a letter direct to NS&I asking for the valuation will suffice.

Premium Bonds

You must notify the Premium Bonds Office of the holder's death. A form for completion is available at www.nsandi.com, or contact National Savings & Investments on 0500 007 007.

Bonds can either be encashed or they can remain in the prize draw for 12 months after the death. If any prize is won, a cheque will usually be sent to the executors, and the prize will belong to the estate to be distributed under the deceased's Will, or the intestacy rules if there is no Will. As long as the value of the bonds and any prize money doesn't exceed £15,000, there is normally no need to provide a copy of the grant of probate or confirmation to receive payment. Premium Bonds are valued at their face value. They should also be listed on the National Savings Form NS&I 904.

Outstanding salary or pension payments

If the deceased was employed at the time of death, a letter must be sent to his employer notifying them of the death and asking whether any salary or other payments are outstanding. However, the employer may need to see a copy of the grant of probate or confirmation before paying such payments to the executors.

If the deceased belonged to a union or trade association, there may be a death benefit payable to his family. Likewise, if the deceased was receiving a pension, the scheme administrator or pension provider must be notified of the death and outstanding pension payments claimed.

Outstanding salary or pension payments should be included in Form IHT400 as an asset of the estate. If the deceased was a member of an occupational pension scheme, a lump sum death benefit may be payable and you should write to the scheme administrator or pension provider to find out if that is the case.

Some benefits payable by an employer or a pension fund may be discretionary and not form part of the deceased's estate on death. This means that they don't pass under the deceased's Will or the intestacy rules and may not be subject to Inheritance Tax. However, HMRC will require full details of all pension payments and lump sum benefits and these should be provided in Schedule IHT409 of Form IHT400.

Life insurance and pension policies

Write to the life insurance company or pension provider to notify them of the date of death, stating the policy number and enclosing a copy of a registrar's copy of the death certificate. Ask what sum is payable on the death and whether it was written in trust for any named person. If it was, the proceeds may be paid direct to that person on production of the death certificate. If not, the proceeds, including any bonuses, will generally be included as part of the deceased's estate and must be included in Schedule IHT410 of Form IHT400. Sometimes, the policy will be linked to a loan or mortgage, in which case the proceeds will be paid directly to the creditor, any excess being paid to the estate. The executor should ask the provider to confirm if the policy is included as part of the estate for Inheritance Tax Purposes.

Taxes and bills

If the deceased paid Income Tax under PAYE (Pay As You Earn system) and/or received interest net of tax on bank or building society accounts, there may be a tax refund to claim. On the other hand, if income has been paid gross, or the deceased was a higher rate taxpayer, there may be additional Income Tax to pay. There may also be Capital Gains Tax to pay if; for example, the deceased sold any shares in the tax year to death. In any event, HMRC must be informed of the death and a tax return completed by the executors, relating to the period up to the date of death.

A refund of Council Tax may be due. In England and Wales, the deceased's home will be exempt from Council Tax if it's left empty from the date of death until probate or confirmation has been granted, and for a further six months from the date of the grant. If the death leaves just one other person living in the property, the 25 per cent discount for single occupation may be claimed from the date of death. Any refund of Council Tax in respect of a period before the date of death must be included in Form IHT400 as an asset of the estate. In Scotland, a Council Tax exemption is available for six months after the date of death, and thereafter the exemption is at the discretion of the local authority.

Social Security payments

In England and Wales, if the deceased was receiving a state retirement pension, the local Department for Work and Pensions office should be notified of the death. The pension book (if there is one) should be sent with your letter inquiring whether there are any pension payments uncollected by the deceased. Any underpaid pension will be a debt due to the deceased and must be included in Form IHT400 as an asset of the estate. If the deceased was receiving any other state benefits, these will also need to be stopped and any outstanding payments due up to the date of death claimed. In Scotland, the Tell Us Once service can be used when registering the death to notify HMRC, DWP, Council Tax office and TV licensing and DVLA.

Foreign property

The value in sterling of property owned by the deceased outside the UK or debts owed to him by any resident outside the UK must be reported to the Probate Registry or HMRC in Schedule IHT417 of Form IHT400. Inheritance Tax can be payable on foreign property if the deceased is domiciled in the UK at the time of death.

Digital assets

The deceased may have owned digital assets, such as cryptocurrency (e.g. Bitcoin). Such assets, although becoming more commonplace, are difficult to access and administer. You should try to locate as much information as you can about such assets, taking care to safeguard any passwords, keys, digital wallets or other login information you find. Seek specialist advice on how to value and transfer these assets.

Applying for a grant

Excepted/exempt estates

To assist with the proper completion of the applications for a grant of probate or confirmation and the appropriate returns to HMRC (to calculate whether Inheritance Tax is due on an estate), it is first necessary for the executors to determine if the estate qualifies as an 'excepted' estate, or as an 'exempt and excepted' estate, or if neither category applies. This will dictate how to complete certain parts of the applications for a grant and which form is to be used to return the relevant IHT information to HMRC.

For deaths prior to 1 January 2022, it is essential on every grant application to complete an IHT form, irrespective of whether IHT is payable. For deaths on or after 1 January 2022, if the deceased's estate is an excepted estate or an excepted and exempt estate there is no requirement to complete an IHT form.

For Inheritance Tax, the value of the estate for probate or confirmation is only one component of the gross estate and if the deceased made substantial gifts during his lifetime, or received income from a substantial trust, or where certain other circumstances apply, this can result in a tax liability even if the IHT tax threshold is not exceeded.

Where the deceased was domiciled in the UK at death, the estate is an 'excepted' estate or an 'exempt and excepted' estate where either:

1. **Excepted estate** – the gross estate for Inheritance Tax does not exceed the excepted estates limit (currently £325,000 and linked to the level of the IHT threshold).

OR

2. **Exempt and excepted estate** – – (a) the gross value of the estate is less than £3,000,000 (£1,000,000 for deaths before 1 January 2022) and (b) because all or part of the estate passes to the deceased's spouse who must also be domiciled in the UK, or to a charity or other body qualifying as exempt from IHT, after deducting liabilities and those exemptions only, the estate is less than the excepted estates limit. Alternatively, the gross value of the estate may be less than or equal to twice the excepted estate limit and a transfer of an unused nil rate band on Form IHT217 is being claimed from the estate of a spouse or civil partner who died before the deceased.

In addition, for both categories all of the following conditions apply:

1. If there are any 'specified transfers' (see below), their total chargeable value does not exceed £250,000 (£150,000 for deaths before 1 January 2022).
2. If the deceased had made a gift of land or buildings, it was made to an individual and not to trustees of a trust or to a company and it did not exceed £250,000 (£150,000 for deaths before 1 January 2022) in chargeable value.
3. If the estate for Inheritance Tax purposes includes assets held in a trust that are treated as part of the deceased's estate, there is only one such trust and the total value of those assets does not exceed £250,000 (£150,000 for deaths before 1 January 2022).
4. If the estate includes any foreign assets, the total gross value of these does not exceed £100,000.
5. The deceased did not give away any property whilst retaining the benefit of it.
6. The deceased had elected that the Income Tax charge should not apply to: (a) assets he previously owned in which he retained a benefit or (b) the deceased's contribution to the purchase price of the assets acquired by another person but in which the deceased retained a benefit.
7. The deceased did not benefit from an alternatively secured pension fund.
8. The deceased did not benefit under a registered pension scheme where (a) the benefit was unsecured and (b) they became entitled to the benefit as a relevant dependant of a person who died aged 75 or over.

   To qualify as 'specified transfers', the assets given away can only be:

   - Cash
   - Quoted stocks and shares
   - Household and personal goods
   - Land and buildings

   Any gift of land and buildings only qualifies as a specified transfer if it was an outright gift between individuals. If the gift of land and buildings was to a trust or a company, or the deceased kept back any kind of benefit from the property or was entitled to use it, it cannot qualify as a specified transfer.

If you are not sure whether any transfers made by the deceased fall within these exceptions, you should contact the HMRC Helpline or seek professional legal advice.

Having determined if the estate qualifies as exempt or exempt and excepted, the executors are now in a position to complete the forms appropriately.

The forms – England and Wales

You can apply for a grant either online or by post. If you decide to apply by post, the form you need to complete will depend on whether or not the deceased left a Will. If the deceased did leave a Will, you will need to complete form PA1P. If he died intestate, you will need to complete form PA1A.

If Inheritance Tax is due on the estate and you have completed form IHT400, you must wait 20 working days from the date you submit the IHT forms to HMRC before applying for the grant.

It used to be the case that the applicants would have to attend an interview at a local probate registry before a grant would be issued. This is no longer the case.

Form PA1P Probate Application Form — if the deceased left a Will

Section A — 'About the Applicant(s)' relates to the person or persons who wish to be detailed on the grant of representation, this will be you, the executor and any other person who is detailed on the Will as an Executor willing and able to act. A maximum of four executors can apply.

Section B2 — the information you provide in this section will be based on your statement of truth and will be stored as a public record; it details the information about the person who has died. You will need to detail information as recorded on the death certificate so it is important you have that to hand.

Section B3 — this pertains to the Will itself and you must send the most recent original and current Will with your application. If you do not send the Will, this delays the application. Be careful not to mark or damage the original Will in any way or, for example, take it apart to photocopy it.

In this section you need to detail important information which addresses issues such as 'Is there anyone under 18 who benefits from the Will?'. If yes, and no named executor is applying for the grant, certain rules apply, in that two people are required to make the application. You will need to contact the Probate Registry in this instance, to see who is entitled to do so.

This section also asks if any of the executors are unable to apply for the grant. The Probate Registry will need to know why. The following reasons will need to be explained.

a) Executor has died before the deceased.

b) Executor has died after the deceased, but before this application is being submitted.

c) Power reserved — the executor has chosen not to apply in section A, but reserves the right to do so later.

d) Renunciation — an executor has renounced the right to apply and has given up all rights to do so; the executor will need to complete a PA15 'renunciation form' which must be supplied with the application.

e) Executor wishes to use a power of attorney to apply on their behalf; if so, a PA11 'attorney form' needs to be supplied with this application. You will need to speak to the Probate Registry in relation to this, as if an attorney is applying for the grant, an executor acting in their own right may not apply jointly for the grant.

f) Executor lacks capacity and is incapable of managing their own affairs; a form PA14 'medical certificate' signed by a GP will need to be sent with the application.

Section B4 — deals with providing information on the relatives of the person who died and the relationship of the executors to the person who has died.

Section B5 — relates to if you are applying as an attorney on behalf of one or more people entitled to apply for the grant; if the person you are acting for lacks capacity under the Mental Capacity Act 2005 and is incapable of managing their affairs you may want to seek legal advice.

Section B6 — relates to foreign domicile, if applicable to the deceased.

Section B7— is in relation to Inheritance Tax and needs to be completed accordingly, alerting the Probate Registry if you have made submission in relation to IHT online or which forms you have completed. You will need to provide figures from the IHT forms (if completed) on PA1P , so it is important to make copies of all forms completed in relation to tax, so you can refer to them if required. If you are not required to submit an IHT form at all, then you will still need to be able to provide figures for the gross and net values of the estate. More information on how to do this can be found online at rb.gy/hhdg2f.

Legal Statement — All persons applying for the grant, as detailed in section A, must sign the statement of truth.

Once you have completed the form, work your way through the checklist on the front of the form to check that you are enclosing all of the relevant documentation.

The fee for applying for a grant is currently £273 and there is a cost of £1.50 for each copy of the grant which you require. Note that if the value of the estate is under £5,000, there is no application fee, although the fee for copies of the grant still applies.

Form PA1A Probate Application Form — if the deceased did not leave a Will

PA1A should also be used where an existing Will does not make adequate provision, or a beneficiary has died and is unable to accept the gift and the Will has not made alternative provision.

Section A — 'About the Applicant(s)' relates to the person or persons who wish to be detailed on the grant, this will be you and any other person who are applying for the grant. If you have any queries on who is entitled to apply for this grant you may want to seek legal advice.

Section B2 — the information you provide here will be based on your statement of truth and will be stored as a public record; it details the information about the person who has died. You will need to detail information as recorded on the death certificate, so it is important you have that to hand. This section also asks questions on if the deceased was married or had any foreign assets.

Section B3 — determines if the deceased has a surviving spouse or civil partner and any blood and adoptive relatives when they died. If any of the applicants are grandchildren of the deceased and their parents are still alive, unless they lack capacity the parents (son or daughter of the deceased) will need to apply. This section is relevant if there is an intestacy (no Will) or a partial intestacy (the Will fails to dispose of all the deceased estate) as it assists in determining who should inherit the deceased assets.

Section B4 — relates to if you are applying as an attorney on behalf of one or more people entitled to apply for the grant of representation; if the person you are acting for lacks capacity under the Mental Capacity Act 2005 and is incapable of managing their affairs you may want to seek legal advice.

Section B5 — relates to foreign domicile, if applicable to the deceased.

Section B6 — is in relation to Inheritance Tax and needs to be completed accordingly alerting the probate registry if you have made submission in relation to IHT online or which forms you have completed. You will need to provide figures from the IHT forms (if completed) on PA1A, so it is important to make copies of all forms completed so you can refer to them if required. If you are not required to submit an IHT form at all then you will still need to be able to provide figures for the gross and net values of the estate. More information on how to do this can be found online at: rb.gy/hhdg2f.

Legal Statement — All persons applying for the grant, as detailed in section A, must sign the statement of truth.

Once you have completed the form, work your way through the checklist on the front of the form to check that you are enclosing all of the relevant documentation.

The fee for applying for a grant is currently £273 and there is a cost of £1.50 for each copy of the grant which you require. Note that if the value of the estate is under £5,000 there is no application fee, although the fee for copies of the grant still applies.

Whichever form you are completing, it needs to be submitted, with the accompanying documentation as set out in the checklist on the front of the form, to HMCTS Probate, PO Box 12625, Harlow CM20 9QE. Make sure you enclose a cheque for the application fee and copies of the grant also. The cheque should be payable to 'HM Courts and Tribunals Service'.

Form IHT205 Short Form of Return of estate information

This form is used where:

* the deceased died on or after 6 April 2011 and before 1 January 2022; and
* the gross value of the estate for IHT is less than the excepted estates limit or is less than £1,000,000 and there is no IHT to pay having regard to the spouse or charity exemptions only.

As you complete IHT205 guidance notes will alert you to the need to complete IHT400 instead, should your answers indicate that IHT is payable. Note that if you need to claim the Residence Nil Rate Band or transferable Residence Nil Rate Band then you must complete an IHT400 rather than an IHT205.

If the deceased was a permanent resident of England or Wales and they estate is an excepted estate then you can complete the online IHT205 rather than a paper form. This is part of the online probate application system which can be accessed via the government's website: https://rb.gy/9sf75g.

The forms – Scotland

Form C1 Confirmation

In every estate where confirmation is needed to 'uplift' or otherwise deal with the deceased's assets, the relevant application form known as Form C1 must be completed by the executor. This form is available to download with this Kit.

Form C1 requires the details of the deceased and the executor(s); the declaration of the executor as to the accuracy of the information contained in the form; an inventory of each item of estate and its value; a summary of the debts and expenses; details of surviving relatives; and a summary of the taxable value of the estate with reference, where appropriate, to the figures contained in Form IHT400 relating to the estate. for deaths on or after 1 January 2022, form C1 Confirmation 2022 should be used. Provided the estate is not taxable, there are no other forms to be completed.

For deaths on or before 31 December 2021, the form C1 Confirmation 2021 should be used. It will also be necessary to complete a C5 form 2006, for deaths on or after 1st September 2006 but before 1st January 2022. Where required, a form IHT217 may also be required. For deaths pre-1 September 2006, please refer to HMRC guidance or seek legal advice.

All versions of the C1 form require a declaration to be made by the executor. This declaration (normally on page 2 of the form) sets out precisely why confirmation in favour of the executors named on page 1 should be granted.

In all cases for taxable estates, the original IHT 400 and schedules should be sent to HMRC, together with a copy of the C1 form. Note. You should not send HMRC the principal C1, as they no longer stamp and return documents. Instead, HMRC now issues a letter of authority to seek confirmation. This letter of authority should be sent to the Court, together with the principal C1, Will and any other relevant documents. All documents being sent to the Court should be the principal documents and should be docquetted. Guidance Notes (Form C3) are available to download with this Kit to assist with completion of Form C1. The estate is not taxable if it qualifies as either an excepted estate, or an exempt and excepted estate, but whether taxable or not, a further form must be completed and submitted to HMRC to allow it to satisfy itself as to the position (see below re Form C5 or Form IHT400).

Form C5 (SE) Information about Small Estates

If the gross value of the deceased's own assets, including his share of jointly held property (but not property passing under a survivorship destination), and including assets that have been nominated to another person during the deceased's lifetime but which are part of the estate (e.g. friendly society funds or a death benefit) is less than £36,000, the estate is called a 'small estate' and the Sheriff Clerk will help you complete Form C1. The executor is not excluded from the benefits of this procedure even if the value of the estate for Inheritance Tax purposes exceeds the small estates limit as a result of lifetime gifts, gifts with reservation, etc. However, even with a small estate, in these circumstances it will still be necessary for the executor to submit the necessary form to HMRC to allow the tax liability to be agreed and Form C5 (SE) is used for this purpose. There are different C5 forms depending on the date of death. If the death was after 1 January 2022, no C5 form is required.

Bond of caution

In the case of an application for confirmation by an executor-dative in an intestate estate, before applying it's normally necessary for a 'bond of caution' to be obtained from an insurance company. This bond of caution is effectively a guarantee given by the insurance company to the court that the executor-dative will distribute the deceased's estate properly in terms of the law of intestate succession. A single premium is payable for such a bond of caution, likely to be around £300 or more, depending on the values and circumstances. In granting such a bond of caution, the insurance company may require certain conditions to be complied with, such as the need to obtain clearance from the Department of Work and Pensions that there has been no overpayment of benefits or that a minor beneficiary's share of the estate should be held until the beneficiary attains the age of 16.

Where the executor-dative is to be the spouse of the deceased, and if the spouse's prior rights exhaust the whole of the intestate estate of the deceased (see page 27), then only the spouse is entitled to seek appointment as executor-dative and there is no requirement for a bond of caution.

The forms – England & Wales and Scotland

Form IHT400 Full Inheritance Tax Return

If the estate is neither excepted, nor exempt and excepted, then Form IHT400 must be completed. HMRC's guidance notes are available to download with this Lawpack Kit. The form comprises 16 pages and separate Schedules numbered IHT401 to IHT421. There are two further schedules for claiming the Residence Nil Rate Band: IHT435 and IHT436. It enables you (and HMRC) to determine whether any Inheritance Tax is payable. The questions on IHT400 are similar to those on IHT205, but they require fuller details. If there is insufficient space for all the information asked for, you should either use the additional information box at the end of the IHT400 form or attach a separate sheet of paper and include the total on Form IHT400 itself. Not every Schedule will require completion, depending on the deceased's circumstances.

If the estate includes land or buildings in the deceased's sole name, Schedule IHT405 should also be completed. If it includes stocks and shares, list the details on Schedules IHT411 and IHT412. Schedules IHT403, IHT418 and IHT409 deal with gifts, assets held in trust and death benefits payable under pension policies respectively. These may not appear to be part of the estate, but they may need to be considered in order to calculate Inheritance Tax. Schedule IHT404 deals with jointly-held property, including land and buildings. Overseas land and buildings and other foreign property should be included in Schedule IHT417.

The Inheritance Tax on some types of property may be paid by instalments. Page 12 of the form includes a box to be ticked, should you wish to do that.

The executors have the choice of either calculating any Inheritance Tax themselves or leaving it to HMRC to work it out.

All the executors should read the Declaration of Form IHT400 and sign it on page 14 once the form and schedules are completed.

Schedule IHT405 Houses, land, buildings and interests in land

Complete this form if the deceased owned a house or any land or rights over land, such as fishing rights, in his sole name; only the total amount will be carried to current Boxes 68 and 70 on Form IHT400. The notes at the top tell you what to put in each column. If the property is let, attach copies of the tenancy agreements.

Under 'Open market value' don't deduct the amount of any mortgage which has been or will need to be repaid. If the deceased owned, for example, the house in his sole name, record the gross value of the entire property, even if the spouse or someone else is claiming an interest in part of it. The debt of the mortgage will be recorded elsewhere on the form.

Schedules IHT411 and IHT412 Stocks and Shares

If the deceased owned stocks or shares, the details of those holdings should be entered in the appropriate Schedules, depending upon whether the assets are UK government securities, listed stocks and shares (not giving control of the company) (use IHT411), or unlisted stocks and shares and control holdings (use IHT412); only the totals from each Schedule are carried to Boxes 62 to 67 on page 8 of Form IHT400.

The Schedules tell you the order in which you should list the holdings and where to show dividends. If you have a professional valuation of the assets, you should include this.

If the deceased was a joint owner of the property, you should complete Schedule IHT404 and include the value of the deceased's share, where requested.

This is by no means an exhaustive discussion of all parts of the Form IHT400 and its Schedules and we have covered only some of the most commonly applicable sections. In the event that you encounter difficulty in completion of the Form, the HMRC Guidance Notes are very helpful, or you may wish to seek professional advice.

Application for confirmation in Scotland

If there is Inheritance Tax (IHT) to pay on a Scottish estate, you will need an IHT reference number and a payslip before you make the payment. Fill in Form IHT422 and send it to the address shown on that form or apply online.

Payment can be submitted by telephone, CHAPS, or online (see www.gov.uk/paying-inheritance-tax) or by post to the HMRC accounts office at:

HM Revenue & Customs
Inheritance Tax
BX9 1AS

Forms IHT400 and a copy of the signed Form C1 should both be submitted in the first instance to:

HM Revenue & Customs
Inheritance Tax
BX9 1AS

A Letter of Authority will be issued by HMRC which will allow the application for confirmation to be submitted to the Sheriff Court.

If you are using the IHT Direct Payment Scheme (DPS) by which the deceased's bank released funds direct to HMRC to meet the tax, complete Form IHT423 and send this to the deceased's bank at the same time.

Application for confirmation is made to the Sheriff Clerk of the Sheriff Court in the area in which the deceased had been domiciled at his death by:

1. Form C1 (receipted where Inheritance Tax is payable).
2. Form C5 (where no tax due and estate is excepted or exempt and excepted) the forms used depending on the date of death.
3. Will ('docketed' with reference to Form C1, i.e. containing a statement linking the Will with the Form) or bond of caution, as appropriate.
4. Letters of declinature from any surviving executor named in the Will and not wishing to accept office (docketed with reference to Form C1).
5. The appropriate fee, currently:

   for a gross estate under £5,000: nil;

   for a gross estate not exceeding £50,000: £271;

   for a gross estate exceeding £50,000: £543.

   A charge of £8 is payable for each certificate of confirmation requested. A certificate of confirmation relates to an individual item of estate and allows multiple certificates to be circulated among asset holders, without the delay in circulating the principal confirmation document among them all.
6. Request for confirmation and any required certificates of confirmation.

Within about two to four weeks after submitting your application for confirmation to the Sheriff Court concerned, the Sheriff Clerk will send to you the confirmation (together with any certificates of confirmation ordered), with the exception of Edinburgh Sheriff Court, which is four to eight weeks. Applications for all the non-Scottish-domiciled deceased (regardless of where they owned property), should be submitted to Edinburgh Sheriff Court.

The grant of confirmation is proof to the public that the executors can realise the deceased's estate, collect from the deceased's debtors and distribute the assets, as determined by the Will. Both the Will and the grant of confirmation are public documents. The executors can now send the confirmation, or a certificate of confirmation, to all parties concerned, requesting whatever money is due to the estate. This money can be deposited into the executors' bank account from which debts of the deceased can be paid.

Inheritance Tax

The executors can calculate the tax themselves by working through the Form IHT400 calculation sheets and completing the Form IHT400 accordingly. If the executors are not sure how to complete Form IHT400, the Inheritance Tax Helpline (tel: 0300 123 1072) can be contacted for assistance in completing the form or visit the HMRC website at www.gov.uk/inheritance-tax.

If the executors don't wish to calculate the tax, HMRC will do this for them (see flowcharts on page 13 for details).

HMRC exempts all assets left to the surviving spouse or to charity, and the first £325,000 (the tax threshold or 'nil rate band') of the estate not left to the spouse or charity (assuming there have been no gifts made by the deceased in the seven-year period prior to death; if there have been any gifts in the seven-year period before death, you should declare these in Schedule IHT403 to Form IHT400).

Any IHT is due within six months of end of month in which the deceased died; otherwise, interest is payable.

Inheritance Tax owed on buildings or land, a business or a share in a business, shares giving a controlling interest in a quoted company and some unquoted shares can, with prior approval, be paid in ten equal annual instalments (although interest is payable on these instalments if the asset is land or buildings and certain types of shares or business interest). Inheritance Tax on other assets must be paid before the grant of probate can be issued and interest is charged on any Inheritance Tax outstanding from the end of the sixth month after the death (except where it's being paid by non-interest bearing instalments).

Allowances and exemptions

Transactions exempt from IHT are;

* transfers between spouse/civil partner
* gifts to charities and political parties

The executors should note that the available IHT threshold may be increased, if it is appropriate, to apply the rules relating to utilising the unused IHT threshold of a predeceasing spouse (the 'transferable nil rate band').

The nil rate band (NRB) threshold for all estates is currently set at £325,000, this means the estate must be above this threshold to pay any IHT on it.

If a spouse dies and has any unused NRB, this unused share of NRB can be added to the surviving spouse's NRB, upon his or her death, thus increasing the total. The increase is calculated by reference to the percentage of the first spouse's unused NRB

Example: Gary died when the NRB was £300,000 and left unused NRB of £150,000. This means that he has only used 50% of his NRB and 50% is unused.

Denise dies and was married to Gary when he died. At the time of Denise's death the NRB is £325,000. Denise's NRB can be increased by 50% (being the unused percentage of Gary's NRB) so Denise's NRB is increased from £325,000 to £487,500.

Residence nil rate band (RNRB)

Residence nil rate band is in addition to the nil rate band allowance of £325,000 and applies to deaths after 6 April 2017. It applies if there is a "qualifying residential interest" and the residence is "closely inherited". Therefore if the deceased leaves their property to children or grandchildren at the time of death (if held in trust this does not apply, subject to very limited exceptions) this additional tax free amount can be added to the basic NRB amount as explained above. If someone dies on or after 6 April 2017 and their estate is above the basic IHT threshold (£325,000), the estate may be entitled to an additional threshold before any IHT becomes due. Note that the RNRB tapers away by £1 for every £2 that the deceased's estate is over £2,000,000.

The RNRB was introduced in phases, with the amount increasing year on year. For deaths:

- Between 6 April 2017 – 5 April 2018: £125,000
- Between 6 April 2018 – 5 April 2019: £150,000
- From 6 April 2019: £175,000.

It is currently due to be fixed at £175,000 until at least 5 April 2026.

In the same way as it is possible to transfer any unused NRB from a previously deceased spouse, it is possible to transfer any unused portion of the RNRB. In cases where the first spouse to die did so before 6 April 2017 then they will be treated as not having used any of their RNRB so potentially the full amount (100%) can be transferred to the estate of the surviving spouse who has subsequently died. You will need to seek legal advice or speak to HMRC to see if this applies.

Example: June dies on 28 August 2018 leaving her estate to four children. Her estate is valued at £650,000, including her home worth £300,000. No other exemptions or reliefs apply and when her husband died, he used up all of his nil rate band and none therefore passes to June. On 28 August 2018 the NRB was £325,000 and the RNRB was £150,000.

Estate value = £650,000

Total RNRB of £300,000 (June's plus her husband's allowance) taxed at 0%.

NRB of £325,00 taxed at 0%.

Remaining £25,000 taxed at 40% = £10,000 IHT to be paid.

Annual exemption

If the total value of all lifetime gifts in any one tax year doesn't exceed £3,000, then they will all be free of Inheritance Tax. If the total value of gifts in any tax year is less than £3,000, then the surplus of this relief can be carried forward to the next tax year only and be used against gifts made in that later tax year, once the £3,000 available for the later tax year has been used up. This relief is known as the annual exemption.

There are also reliefs such as Business Relief and Agricultural Relief. We suggest you speak to a legal advisor or HMRC if you are unsure if these or any of the above apply.

Changes to the amount of Inheritance Tax

Even after probate or confirmation has been granted, HMRC may ask further questions about the assets and liabilities of the estate, and values may have to be negotiated. For example, HMRC may challenge the value reported on Form IHT400 for a house or for unquoted shares. This could result in more Inheritance Tax being payable.

If the executors discover an asset or debt of the deceased which they didn't know about before they applied for probate or confirmation, they must report it to HMRC as soon as possible after its discovery. This may also change the amount of Inheritance Tax payable.

Once the Inheritance Tax position has been settled, the executors should ask HMRC for Form IHT30, an application for a 'clearance certificate' confirming the executors to be discharged from further Inheritance Tax. A copy, completed and signed by all the executors, should be send to HMRC. HMRC will then issue a clearance certificate (SL120). The executors can then distribute the estate. However, if any further assets come to light subsequently, these too will need to be reported to HMRC, as the discharge from Inheritance Tax would not cover them or the situation where a further tax liability arises from a deed varying the disposition of the estate.

Raising money to pay Inheritance Tax and the probate fee or confirmation dues

Because an executor cannot draw on the funds in the deceased's bank account until he can show entitlement by producing the grant, the executor may need to borrow the necessary funds to pay Inheritance Tax and the probate fee or confirmation dues. There are, however, some assets which an institution may be willing to release before the grant of probate or confirmation is available, in order to pay the Inheritance Tax, and some assets that may be realised without producing the grant of probate or confirmation. The tax may be covered, or partly covered, from such sources as an alternative to borrowing. The following are assets which the executors may be able to use in this way.

1. **National Savings.** If the deceased had a National Savings account, National Savings certificates or Premium Bonds, National Savings may remit funds direct from the deceased's holdings to HMRC to cover the Inheritance Tax payable on the estate or part of it. You should contact NS&I

directly to enquire about this option either by telephone (0500 007 007) or by writing to NS&I, Glasgow, G58 1SB.

Any remaining balance on the deceased's National Savings account will be paid to the executors and any remaining National Savings certificates and Premium Bonds can be encashed once the grant has been obtained.

2. **Funds payable to others without grant of probate or confirmation.** (see 'Is a grant of probate or confirmation necessary?' on page 9). Consider utilising funds from nominated property, joint property or lump-sum death benefits from pension funds, life assurance companies and friendly societies which have been written in trust for another person. However, such funds or assets would belong to the person to whom they are payable, rather than to the estate, and the executors would need to borrow from that person if they wished to use those funds to pay the Inheritance Tax.
3. **Pension funds and friendly societies.** Funds of up to £5,000 from some pension funds and friendly societies.
4. **Banks and building societies.** Banks and Building societies are often willing to release money to pay Inheritance Tax and the probate fee or confirmation dues, and may have agreed to be part of HMRC's Direct Payment Scheme ('DPS'). The executors should complete the DPS form IHT423 and submit one such form to every bank from which funds are required. You must first obtain an IHT reference number from HMRC to include on the form, to ensure that the funds are correctly allocated to the deceased's IHT record. When HMRC receive the funds from the bank(s) they will link this with the IHT400 submitted by the executors and will stamp and return the Probate summary (or in Scotland, Form C1).
5. **Other assets.** Furniture and other personal possessions of the deceased may be sold by executors, who are entitled to sell the assets of the estate from the date of death, but not by administrators in England and Wales, who are only entitled to do so once they have the grant of letters of administration.
6. **Stocks and shares.** If held through a stockbroker's nominee company, subject to the stockbroker's agreement.

If insufficient assets are realisable before the grant is issued, the executors will have to borrow the money to pay the Inheritance Tax. Some sources might include:

1. **Loan from the deceased's bank.** A bank will normally make a loan to the executors, although a fee will be payable based on the size of the loan and, of course, interest will be charged. The executors may claim Income Tax relief on the interest payment for the first year of the administration in respect of a loan for the Inheritance Tax payable on personal property.
2. **Loan from a beneficiary.** A beneficiary may be able and willing to lend the money to the estate to pay the Inheritance Tax, particularly if the bank interest and fee would be paid out of cash that he would otherwise receive.
3. **Loan from HMRC.** This should only be considered as a last resort.

Administering an estate

Distribution of gifts and legacies

To satisfy any debts of the estate, it's the assets forming part of the residuary estate that are used first unless there is a contrary intention expressed in the Will. If there are still outstanding debts when the residuary estate has been used up, cash legacies are reduced proportionately to meet the debt. If there are unpaid debts outstanding, specific items left as legacies under the Will need to be sold. Once all the debts are paid and the assets are all accounted for and collected the executors are in a position to distribute the estate in accordance with the Will.

As each personal effect, gift and legacy of money is distributed to the beneficiaries of the estate, the executors should ask each beneficiary to sign a receipt. The receipt should record the amount of money or description of the gift, the names of the executors, the name and signature of the beneficiary and the date. The beneficiary should be invited to keep a copy of the receipt. The Will may contain a clause saying that, if there is a gift to a child, his parent or guardian can sign the receipt. Otherwise, gifts to minors should be invested by the executor in an account until the child reaches 18 or 16 in Scotland (the age of 'majority') or the age of inheritance specified in the Will, which could be higher.

Transfer of assets

If assets are to be transferred to a beneficiary (rather than being sold and the proceeds paid to him), the method of transfer will differ according to the asset. Household and personal effects may be physically handed over, without any legal paperwork.

Shares will need to be transferred using a Stock Transfer Form (available from www.lawpack.co.uk or by request from the relevant company registrar's office). This should be completed and signed by all executors and sent to the registrar of the company, together with the share certificate and an office copy of the grant of probate, or certificate of confirmation, as appropriate. Alternatively, a stockbroker or bank would be able to prepare the stock transfer forms and send them to the registrars. If a shareholding is to be split between two or more beneficiaries, a separate form of stock transfer is needed for each beneficiary. No stamp duty is payable on the transfer of shares from executors to a beneficiary, provided that the appropriate certificate on the back of the form has been completed and signed by the executors. If the shares are registered in the name of a stockbroker's or bank's nominee company, the executors need not complete stock transfer forms but should write to the nominee company, giving it the name and address of the beneficiary of the shares and instructing it to hold the shares on behalf of the beneficiary in future.

If a house or flat is to be transferred to a beneficiary, the procedure in England and Wales differs according to whether the title is registered or unregistered.

In the case of registered land title(s) in England and Wales, you need to use Land Registry Form AS1 Assent of Whole of Registered Title(s). If only part of the registered land title is being transferred, you will need to complete a Form AS3. Forms are available from www.landregistry.gov.uk. The completed form needs to be signed by each executor in the presence of a witness and by the beneficiary to whom the property is being transferred. The executors should then send it, together with an office copy of the grant of probate, and the Land Registry fee to the Land Registry so they can register the new owner. The Land Registry fee will vary according to the value of the property, net of any outstanding mortgage (if it has not been repaid following the death). The current scale of fees for registering an assent is as follows:

Value net of mortgage	Fee
£0 – £100,000	£45
£100,001 – £200,000	£70
£200,001 – £500,000	£100
£500,001 – £1,000,000	£145
£1,000,001 and over	£305

The Land Registry will also want verification of identity of the new owners (i.e. beneficiaries) of the property, and form ID1 should be completed for each new owner.

If the land is in England and Wales and is unregistered, the title deeds will consist of a number of deeds and documents including the deed (a 'conveyance') whereby the property was transferred to the deceased. In the case of unregistered land it's best to seek the advice of a solicitor as the title to the property would then have to be registered at the Land Registry as a first registration application in order for it to be put into the names of the beneficiaries.

In Scotland, whether the title of heritable property (i.e. land or buildings) is registered in the Land Register of Scotland or not, a 'docket' on the confirmation or certificate of confirmation can be a method of transferring title to a beneficiary (either under a Will or in terms of legal rights, or in accordance with the law of intestate succession in Scotland). The confirmation or certificate of confirmation with completed docket should be held with the titles of the property. It may be prudent for preservation purposes to have the docketed confirmation (or certificate of confirmation) registered in the Books of Council and Session on application to:

The Keeper of the Registers of Scotland
Meadowbank House
153 London Road
Edinburgh EH8 7AU

A docket isn't needed if the title deed contains a survivorship destination, as the title will automatically have transferred to the survivor on the death of the first to die.

It should be noted that a docket will suffice as a 'link in title' to allow the beneficiary to sell the asset at a later date, or bequeath it under his own Will, but as the beneficiary's title has not been registered in the Land Register of Scotland, there may be problems at a later date if, for example, the beneficiary wishes to use the property as security for a loan. If the beneficiary wishes to ensure that the entitlement is a matter of public record and that all the usual benefits of full ownership apply, the beneficiary may prefer that the executors execute a formal disposition in his favour instead of a docket. This will incur registration dues (based on the property value) when the disposition is registered in the Land Register, but this would normally be treated as an expense of the estate.

Final accounts

The careful records that have been kept since the date of death should now be organised in a neat and easily-read format for approval by each beneficiary.

A word of caution: In England and Wales, for a period of six months following the grant of probate, claims may be made under the Inheritance (Provision for Family and Dependants) Act 1975. A claim might be made, for example, by a member of the deceased's family who feels he has not been properly provided for in the Will. In England and Wales, it's therefore wise not to distribute the residue of the estate until six months have passed. If such a claim is made, the executors should seek the advice of a solicitor.

In Scotland, it may also be prudent to delay distribution of the estate until six months after the death to allow for any claims to be made against the estate. If the executor were to distribute before the expiry of that six-month period, he may be personally liable for any claims made in that period. Additionally, where a deceased died intestate while cohabiting unmarried, or in a relationship with the same characteristics except that the parties were of the same sex, it is open to the cohabitee to make a claim against the estate within six months of the date of death. If such a claim is foreseeable, the executors should not consider distributing the estate to other beneficiaries within that period.

After the residuary beneficiaries (or those entitled under the intestacy laws) have signed off on the accounts, the estate is completed. The executors' bank account can be closed and whatever money remains is given to those entitled under the Will or intestacy laws.

Paperwork should be kept on file for 12 years after final distribution. In the event that the deceased left someone a life interest or liferent in the estate, or the Will created any other form of ongoing trust, the paperwork should be kept for 12 years after the final distribution to whoever inherits after the death of the last person with a life interest or liferent.

In Scotland, the principal papers such as the deceased's Will, confirmation, final accounts and beneficiaries' receipts should ideally be retained indefinitely, particularly where there is a continuing trust. It is a requirement to keep records for 20 years.

Taxation of the estate

Income from the estate will be liable to Income Tax from the date of death to the date it has been fully administered. The estate will be assessed to Income Tax on all income received gross at the basic rate, but with no personal allowance. No further Income Tax will be payable if all income (e.g. bank interest, dividends) has been paid net of tax. Gains (relative to date of death values) on any sales of shares after death may be liable to Capital Gains Tax. The executors' annual exemption for Capital Gains Tax is the same as any individual's annual exemption for the tax year in which the death occurred and the following two years. However, gains in an estate are taxed at higher, rather than basic, rates (28 per cent for residential property and 20% for all other chargeable gains). Thus the executors should liaise with the beneficiaries before selling assets which are likely to make a taxable gain to see whether the

Capital Gains Tax can be reduced by using the beneficiaries' rates of tax and exemptions. If in doubt, the executors should seek professional advice.

Having been notified of the death, HMRC will assess whether the deceased had an outstanding lifetime Income Tax and/or Capital Gains Tax liability or if he had overpaid. In order to assess this, HMRC may request information from the executors. HMRC will either issue a tax repayment, or request that a full self-assessment return is made for the deceased for the tax year to date of death in order to assess any tax due.

The executors may also need to issue a certificate of tax deduction Form R185 (Estate Income), also available from the tax office and the gov.uk website, to the beneficiary who is entitled to the residue of the estate. This form shows the gross income received by the estate during the tax year, the tax paid by the executors on that income and the resulting net figure. As long as the residue isn't held in trust, the income of the estate is treated as the income of the beneficiary, who will report the income on his tax return, and Form R185 (Estate Income) is evidence that tax has already been paid on it. If the beneficiary is a non-taxpayer, he can reclaim the tax. If he is a higher or additional rate taxpayer, he will be assessable to additional tax. An accountant will be best placed to advise on this.

Succession on intestacy

If a person dies without making a Will, or if their Will is invalid, they die intestate. The management of their estate, which is their house (if any) and other assets minus their debts and liabilities, is then placed in the hands of administrators (called executors-dative in Scotland) appointed by the court, who are likely to be close members of the deceased's family.

It is also possible for someone to die partially intestate. This occurs if a testator fails to deal with all of their property in their Will, or if a beneficiary dies before the testator and they haven't provided for that contingency. If any part of the inheritance cannot be given to another beneficiary named under the Will, that part must be distributed according to the laws of intestacy.

Legislation covering intestacy in the three UK jurisdictions is:

- the Administration of Estates Act 1925 in England and Wales;
- the Succession (Scotland) Act 1964, as amended by the Law Reform Miscellaneous Provisions (Scotland) Act 1968 and Succession (Scotland) Act 2016, in Scotland.

These Acts apply to anyone whose domicile or permanent home at the time of death is in a particular jurisdiction, or in some cases to someone whose home is abroad but who retains domicile in the particular jurisdiction.

In effect, these rules allow the deceased's surviving spouse and dependants to claim their property and money without regard to any verbal expression of wishes the deceased may have made. Only by making a Will can a testator ensure that his wishes will be carried out on death. If no surviving relatives can be found, the deceased's entire estate goes to the Crown as what is known as *bona vacantia.*

In Scotland a mistress, common-law wife, spouse separated by a formal separation agreement which must revoke rights to each others' estate and revoke prior and legal rights and a divorced spouse have no right to inherit under the laws of intestacy (except as previously stated in Scotland where a cohabitee may potentially have a claim on an intestate estate). In England and Wales, a spouse separated by a decree of judicial separation takes no benefit under the laws of intestacy.

Rules of intestacy in England and Wales

The rules of intestacy are complex. The effect of the rules depends partly on the size of the deceased's estate. If the estate is large, less may go to the spouse than expected. Broadly speaking, funeral expenses and administration costs are deducted from the estate. The remaining property is distributed as follows:

1. If only the deceased's spouse survives them, he receives all of the property remaining in the estate, provided that he survives for 28 days after their spouse's death.
2. If the spouse survives the deceased by 28 days and the deceased is also survived by issue:
   a) the surviving spouse receives:
      i) a 'statutory legacy' of up to £322,000, plus interest accrued from the time of death until payment — the statutory legacy is free from tax and costs (for deaths prior to 26 July 2023 the statutory legacy was £270,000);
      ii) all household and personal items of the deceased ('personal chattels'); and
      iii) half of any surplus over the £322,000.
   b) the children receive:
      i) the other half of the remaining estate divided equally among them;
3. Under the Inheritance and Trustees Powers Act, for deaths on or after 1 October 2014, if the spouse survives the deceased by 28 days and, instead of children, there are parents, brothers, sisters, nieces and/or nephews, none of them inherits and the surviving spouse takes the whole estate. For deaths before 1 October 2014, different rules apply and professional advice should be sought.
4. If there is no surviving spouse but there are surviving children, the estate is divided equally among the children (if any of the children have died before the deceased, leaving their own child/children, those child/children will automatically take their parent's share by substitution):
   a) they inherit immediately if they have achieved the age of 18 or are married.
   b) the estate is held in trust for minor children until they reach the age of 18 or marry.
5. If there is no surviving spouse or children, but the deceased is survived by his parents, they receive absolute title to the entire estate to be divided equally between them.

6. If there is no surviving spouse, children or parents, the estate is inherited in the following order:

   a) brothers and sisters equally, or their issue equally, if none.

   b) half-brothers and half-sisters equally, or their issue equally, if none.

   c) grandparent(s) equally.

   d) uncles and aunts of whole blood equally, or their issue equally, if none.

   e) uncles and aunts of half blood equally, or their issue equally, if none.

   f) the Crown.

Rules of intestacy in Scotland

The rules of intestate succession in Scotland are complex and apply to the estate of anyone who was domiciled in Scotland at their date of death that is not dealt with by a valid Will. If you are in any doubt as to the deceased's domicile for succession purposes, you should seek legal advice. The debts of the estate and the entitlements of beneficiaries under the intestate rules are paid or satisfied either from the 'heritable estate' (land and buildings) or from 'moveable' assets (cash, shares, insurance policies, motor vehicles, etc.) or in some cases, proportionately from both types of asset.

In order to identify which part of the estate must bear the liability for particular debts and to calculate the rights of the relevant parties, the executors must correctly identify which assets are heritable and which are moveable. They then settle all debts and account for the net estate (the estate after payment of debts and expenses) to the beneficiaries under intestacy appropriately.

In addition to the family of the person who dies intestate, there may be a further beneficiary to consider who is the intestate's cohabitee where the intestate (whether also married or not) was cohabiting with a partner at date of death. Legislation allows a cohabitee to apply to the court for provision on the death of the intestate if an application is made within six months of the death. Unlike the rights of family which arise on intestacy as a matter of law, the cohabitee has no automatic right and must make an application to the court. This is known as a section 29 claim under the Family Law (Scotland) Act 2006.

Six steps of administering an intestate estate

Step 1 – Payment of debts

'Moveable debts' (e.g. funeral expenses, legal fees, credit card bills, unsecured loans and expenses incurred up to the point of obtaining confirmation in favour of the executors) are paid out of moveable assets; 'heritable debts' (e.g. a mortgage secured on the home) are paid out of heritable assets. You will see that moveable debts reduce the value of the estate available to 'legal rights' claimants, and heritable debts reduce the value of the estate available to any 'prior rights' claimant, discussed below.

Step 2 – Spouse's prior right to dwellinghouse

The spouse is entitled to the deceased's share of the 'dwellinghouse' (i.e. a house or flat, including garden ground, garage, etc.) in which the spouse was usually resident at the date of the deceased's death, up to the value of £473,000, subject to any 'burdens' affecting it, such as a mortgage. Say the deceased was the sole owner of the house and it is worth £250,000 and it is subject to a mortgage in the deceased's name of £50,000, the value to be used for prior rights purposes is £200,000. That amount, being less than the maximum prior rights value of £473,000, means that the spouse inherits the house. If the house and the mortgage are in joint names of the deceased and the spouse, it is the value of the deceased's share of the house and his share of the debt which are used for the purposes of calculating the value of the prior rights.

If the value of the deceased's interest in the dwellinghouse for prior rights purposes (i.e. after deduction of the value of any heritable debt) is more than £300,000, the spouse does not inherit the house and the entitlement is to cash of £473,000. This could mean the property might have to be sold in order to meet the cash requirement, or if the spouse wished to retain the house, and if the executors agreed, he could reimburse the estate for the excess value of the house over the £473,000 limit.

If the spouse was usually resident in more than one property (e.g. town flat and country house), he has six months from the death to declare his entitlement.

If there is any dispute as to the value of the property, legislation provides for it to be fixed by one arbiter chosen by agreement, or by the Sheriff of the area in which the deceased was domiciled.

Step 3 – Spouse's prior right to furniture and plenishings

This entitlement relates to the value of the deceased's share of any moveable household goods, including articles of furniture, paintings, books, and other items of domestic, household, garage, or garden use, up to the value of £29,000. Motor vehicles would not generally be classed as part of the furniture and plenishings. It is wise for executors to have all items professionally valued, for succession as well as potential tax liability purposes.

Where the value does not exceed £29,000, the spouse is entitled to all. If the value exceeds this figure, the spouse may select items he wishes to have up to that value.

Items used at date of death for business purposes are excluded, as are 'heirlooms' of the deceased's family, defined as 'any article which has associations with the deceased's family of such nature and extent that it ought to pass to some member of the family other than the surviving spouse'.

If the spouse was usually resident in more than one property at the death of the deceased, he is entitled to choose which property the items come from. This need not necessarily be the same property chosen by the spouse for the purposes of the dwellinghouse entitlement. The spouse must choose which house the furniture and plenishings come from within six months of the death.

The right to furniture and plenishings can arise even where the deceased did not own the property in which they are located; for example, the property may be owned solely by the surviving spouse. In this case, the surviving spouse remains entitled to claim the right to the deceased's share of furniture and plenishings in that property, even though the deceased left no interest in a dwellinghouse for the surviving spouse to inherit.

Succession on intestacy in England and Wales

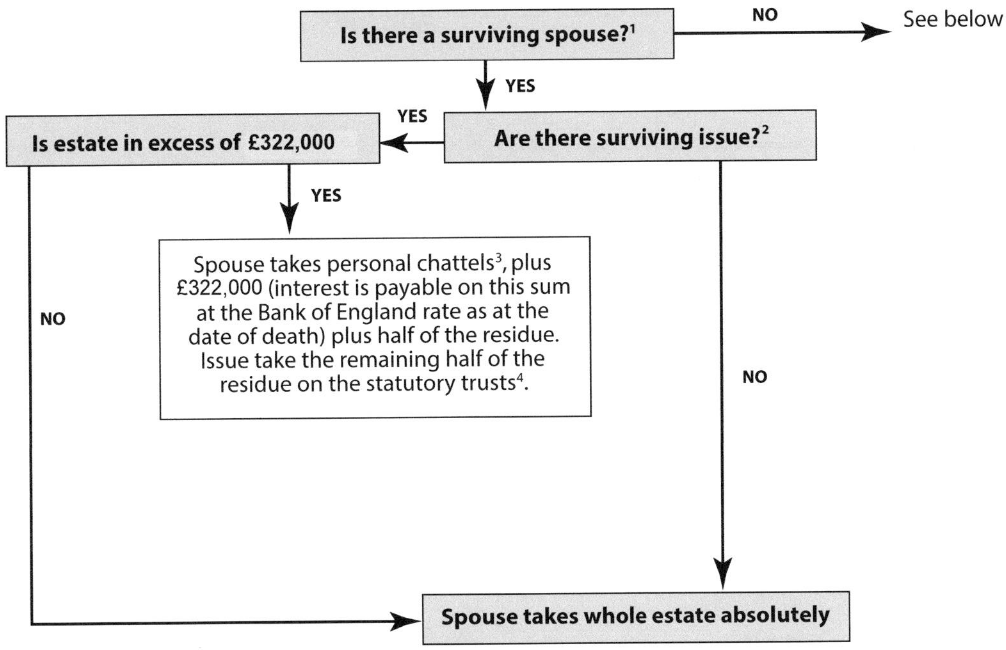

1 The spouse must have survived the deceased by 28 days to inherit.

2 'ISSUE' Children, grandchildren or remoter lineal descendants of the intestate.

3 'PERSONAL CHATTELS' means tangible movable property, but not money or securities for money, or property used at the death of the intestate solely or mainly for business purposes, or property held at the death of the intestate solely as an investment.

4 'THE STATUTORY TRUSTS' Those children of the intestate who are alive at his or her death inherit in equal shares although if a child is under 18 he or she must reach the age of 18 or marry under that age in order to inherit. If any child dies before the intestate, leaving children of his or her own, those children (i.e. the intestate's grandchildren) will take per stirpes i.e. they will take their parents' share equally between them (provided they reach the age of 18 or marry under that age). If remoter issue predeceased the intestate leaving their own issue, this process would continue down the generations. References to the children of the intestate should be read as references to brothers, sisters, aunts or uncles as appropriate, where any of those classes are stated to inherit on the statutory trusts. See illustration of per stirpes distribution on page 26.

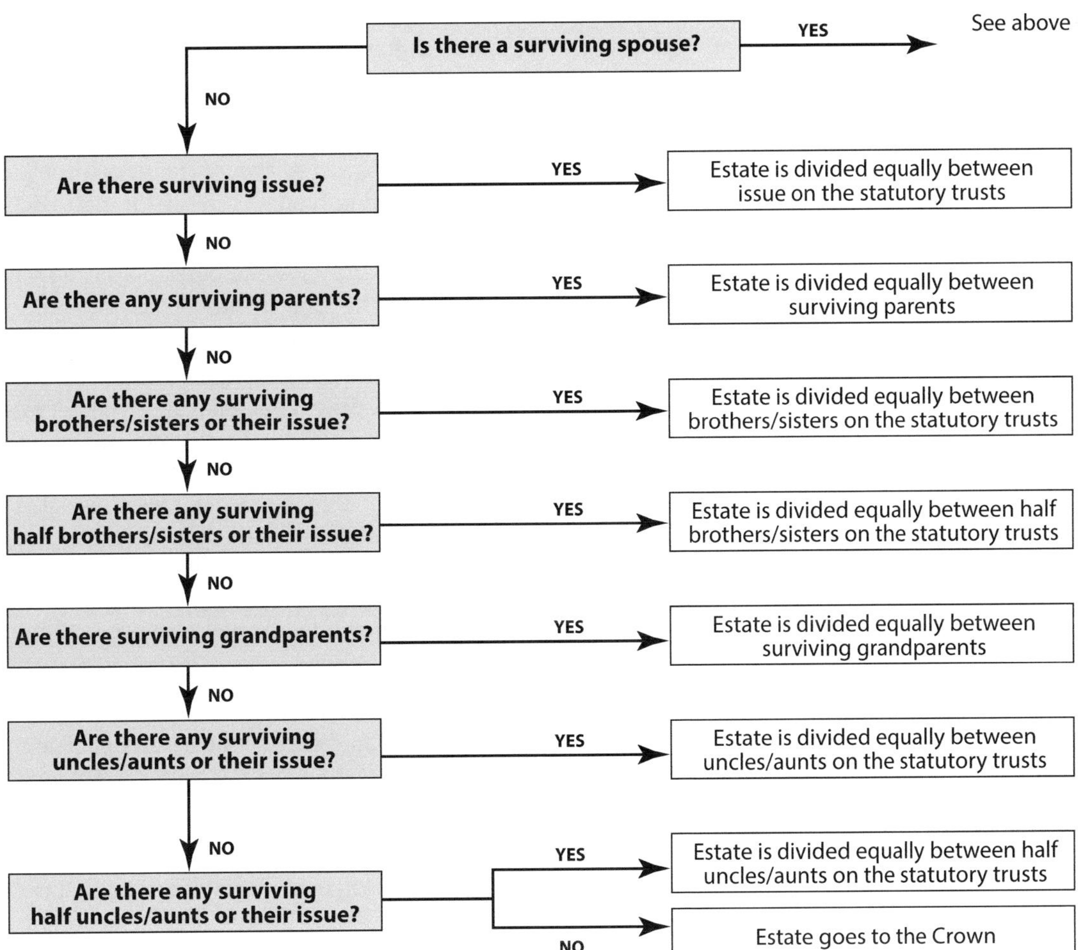

Succession on intestacy in England and Wales (continued)

Illustration of per stirpes distribution (ignoring inheritance tax)

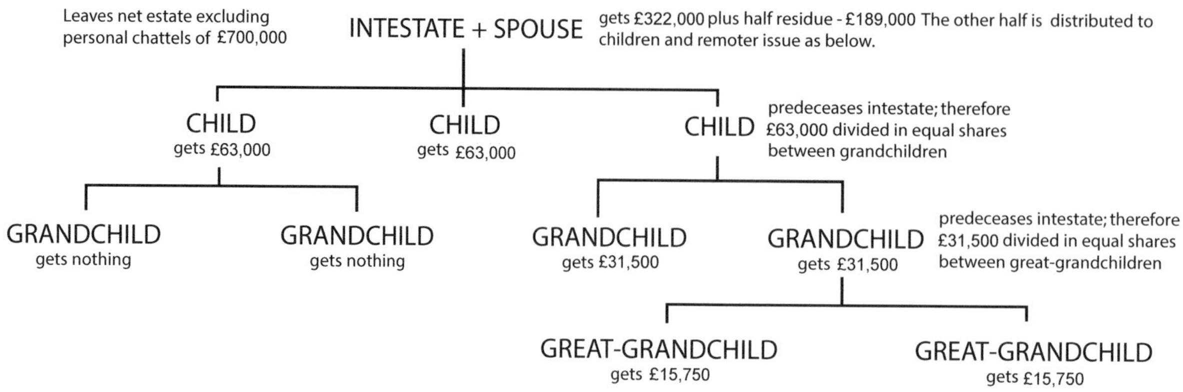

NOTES

1. **Representation**
   Where any person who, if he/she had survived the intestate, would have had right to any part of the intestate estate has predeceased the intestate but has left issue who survive, such issue shall have their parent's right to the estate.
2. **Succession of collaterals (brothers and sisters)**
   Where brothers and sisters of an intestate, or of an ancestor of an intestate have right to any part of the intestate estate, collaterals of the full blood shall be entitled to succeed in preference to collaterals of the half blood. Where collaterals of the half blood succeed, they rank without distinction as between those related to the intestate through their father or their mother.
3. **Succession in cases of illegitimacy**
   No distinction is drawn between succession by legitimate or illegitimate issue of the intestate.

The two rights are entirely independent of each other.

If there is any dispute as to what should be included in this category, legal advice should be sought, and any dispute over value should be referred to arbitration.

Step 4 –Spouse's prior right to cash sum

If the deceased leaves issue (i.e. children and grandchildren), the surviving spouse is entitled to a maximum cash sum of £50,000; if there are no issue, the maximum is £89,000. Naturally, this sum is payable only if there is sufficient cash/assets in the estate; otherwise, it is reduced to the sum that is available. The sum is to be satisfied proportionately from the value of the moveable and heritable estate remaining after satisfaction of prior rights in steps 2 and 3 if both types of estate remain. Otherwise, the cash would be taken only from whatever type of estate remains, whether it is heritable or moveable. This could require the sale of assets from both types of estate. Interest is payable on the cash sum from the date of death to the date of payment at the rate of 7 per cent.

If the value of the intestate estate is not sufficient to meet the prior rights, the surviving spouse may be entitled to the whole intestate estate and this is not uncommon in smaller estates. A divorced spouse or former civil partner has no entitlement to prior rights.

Step 5 – Legal rights of spouse and issue

After satisfaction of prior rights, the executors must then attend to a separate category of rights known as legal rights which are paid from the balance remaining of the deceased's net moveable assets (everything apart from land and buildings) after deduction of any moveable assets used to satisfy any prior rights claim of a spouse (the 'legal rights fund').

If the spouse and issue survive, the legal rights fund is divided in the following manner:

a) one-third to the deceased's spouse;
b) one-third to the deceased's issue (their children and the issue of predeceasing children);
c) one-third is included in the 'free estate' referred to below.

If the deceased leaves no spouse, but does leave issue, then half of the legal rights fund is due to the deceased's issue. The remaining half is included in the 'free estate' referred to below.

If the deceased leaves no issue, but does leave a spouse, then half of the legal rights fund is due to the deceased's spouse. The remaining half is included in the free estate referred to below.

It should be noted that legal rights apply to cases where there is a valid Will, as well as to intestate cases. The deceased may make a Will which excludes his spouse and/or children, but they can if they wish claim their entitlement to legal rights and it is the executors' duty to inform any potential claimant of their rights. However, in cases of a valid Will in which the legal rights claimant has been left a legacy, the claimant must choose between legal rights and the legacy, and may not have both. With these rights in place, it is virtually impossible for a testator to prevent any benefit passing to his spouse or children.

There is an allowance of 20 years for a claim to be made following death and executors have an obligation to make the children aware of the claim and of their rights.

Step 6 – Free estate

After satisfaction of all prior rights and legal rights, what is left in the estate (being the balance of any heritable and moveable property not due in satisfaction of prior rights or legal rights) is

Succession on intestacy in Scotland

STEP 1 All heritable and moveable debts are paid off. Beneficiaries' respective entitlements are shown after all heritable and moveable debts have been deducted

PRIOR RIGHTS OF SPOUSE Payable from heritable and moveable estate

- **STEP 2** House up to £473,000
- **STEP 3** Furniture and plenishings up to £29,000
- **STEP 4** Cash sum of £50,000 **or** £89,000
  - **Do both spouse and issue survive?**
    - YES: Spouse entitled to cash up to £50,000
    - NO: Spouse entitled to cash up to £89,000

STEP 5 **LEGAL RIGHTS OF SPOUSE & ISSUE**
Payable from moveable estate

Do both spouse and issue survive?

- YES: Spouse entitled to 1/3 of NME and issue entitled to 1/3 of NME; remaining 1/3 to free estate
- NO: Spouse entitled to 1/2 of NME if no issue and issue entitled to 1/2 of NME if no spouse; remaining 1/2 to free estate

STEP 6 **FREE ESTATE**
Payable from balance of heritable and moveable estates after deduction of prior and legal rights

	YES →
Are there surviving issue?	Estate is divided equally between issue
NO ↓ **Are there any surviving parents and surviving brothers/sisters?**	Estate is divided one-half to surviving parents and one-half to surviving brothers/sisters
NO ↓ **Are there any surviving brothers/sisters or their issue?**	Estate is divided equally between brothers/sisters or their issue
NO ↓ **Are there any surviving parents?**	Estate is divided equally between surviving parents
NO ↓ **Is there a surviving spouse?**	Estate passes wholly to surviving spouse
NO ↓ **Are there surviving uncles/aunts or their issue?**	Estate is divided equally between uncles/aunts or their issue
NO ↓ **Are there surviving grandparents?**	Estate is divided equally between surviving grandparents
NO ↓ **Are there surviving brothers/sisters of grandparents?**	Estate is divided equally between brothers/sisters of grandparents
NO ↓ **Are there surviving ancestors more remote than grandparents?**	Estate is divided equally between such remoter ancestors, generation by generation, subject to the brothers and sisters of such remoter ancestors having right to the estate before the ancestors of the next remote generation
NO ↓ **If no person is entitled to succeed, the estate falls to the Crown as *ultimus haeres***	

NOTE: Net Moveable Estate is abbreviated to 'NME'

referred to as the free estate. Effectively, this is the part of the deceased's estate he would have been free to dispose of by Will, or which otherwise passes under the rules of intestate succession. The order of succession to the free estate is as follows, with the entitlement passing to the next in line only if there is no one surviving in the earlier categories to inherit:

a) if children or remoter issue survive the deceased, they take the whole intestate estate.

b) if both (i) the deceased's parent(s) and (ii) any brothers or sisters survive, the surviving parent(s) take one half of the free estate and the surviving brother(s) and sister(s) the other half.

c) if brothers and sisters survive but not parents, they take the whole free estate.

d) if parents but not brothers and sisters survive, the parents take the whole free estate.

e) if a spouse survives he will take the whole free estate.

f) if uncles and aunts survive (being brothers and sisters of either parent of the deceased), they take the whole free estate.

g) if a grandparent or grandparents survive (being a parent or parents of either parent of the deceased), they take the whole free estate.

h) if brothers and sisters of any grandparent survive, they take the whole free estate.

i) if there are no survivors under the above categories, then ancestors of the deceased remoter than grandparents, generation by generation successively, without distinction between maternal and paternal lines, shall take the whole of the free estate. Failing ancestors of any generation, the brothers and sisters of those ancestors have right to the free estate, before ancestors of the next more remote generation.

j) if no-one survives under the above categories, then the free estate will go to the Crown.

Note re the above: if there are relatives on the same line who are full- and half-blood, the executors should seek legal advice.

The following principles also apply to the succession to an intestate estate in Scotland:

- Representation applies at every level, so that if no primary beneficiary survives but leaves issue surviving the intestate, such issue will take the parent's share; and only if there is no issue, will the share pass to the next category of beneficiary. If all those inheriting are in the same degree of relationship to the intestate, the inheritance is divided among them equally. If the estate falls to beneficiaries of differing degrees of relationship to the intestate, e.g. a child and two grandchildren (the issue of a predeceasing child), then in this example the intestate's surviving child as the beneficiary nearest in degree would take one-half of the entitlement and the remaining one-half would be divided due equally between the two grandchildren .
- The preference for succession through the male line no longer exists.
- 'Collaterals' (i.e. brothers and sisters) of the full blood will inherit in preference to collaterals of the half blood.

An overview of probate/confirmation

1. Find and review the deceased's Last Will & Testament or establish if the deceased died intestate; and in Scotland identify the beneficiaries on intestacy or any beneficiaries with a legal rights entitlement in a testate estate.

2. Determine who the personal representatives are and whether they are able and willing to act. If not, or if the deceased didn't leave a valid Will, determine who will act as personal representatives. Get the agreement of the personal representatives in writing.

3. Register the death and obtain copies of the death certificate.

4. Attend to the funeral, burial, cremation, etc.

5. Secure the house and/or other property of the deceased, insuring the house, car and any other valuable items as necessary.

6. In England and Wales, obtain forms required online.

7. Organise yourself for valuing assets, corresponding with others, keeping financial records and receiving the deceased's mail. Open an executors' bank account.

8. Write to all financial and business organisations in which the deceased had an interest. Include a copy of the death certificate and request the necessary information for the probate or confirmation application and the returns to HMRC.

9. List the deceased's assets and liabilities. Review them. Is it necessary to apply for a grant of probate or confirmation? If the estate appears to be insolvent or there are other complexities, see a solicitor.

10. If the estate appears to be worth more than £325,000, (or where it exceeds the higher value available after application of a predeceasing spouse's available Inheritance Tax allowance) make arrangements to raise money (e.g. by borrowing or selling some of the deceased's personal property) for Inheritance Tax, which must be paid before the grant of probate or confirmation can be issued. Consider raising the funds from the deceased's own account using the Inheritance Tax Direct Payment Scheme.

11. Fill out probate or confirmation forms as information is collected and return them to the Probate Registry or Sheriff Court concerned. In Scotland, the form of application for confirmation is a Form C1. Depending on when the deceased passed died, complete a Form C5 (in Scotland) or a Form IHT205 (in England and Wales) if the estate is either excepted or exempt and excepted. However, if the estate is neither an excepted estate nor an exempt and excepted estate, then it's necessary for Form IHT400 to be completed and submitted to HMRC prior to applying for confirmation or grant of probate.

12. a) In England and Wales, fill out probate forms as information is collected. Once the form is completed ensure it is signed by all the applicants and send it to the Probate Registry along with the original Will, any codicils, a death certificate and any other documentation required.

b) In Scotland, it is not necessary for the executors to attend at the Sheriff Court concerned as one of the executors can complete the necessary Form C1 which is the application for confirmation and mail it to the Sheriff Court concerned. If the deceased didn't leave a Will, then normally it's necessary for a bond of caution (an insurance indemnity) to be obtained from an insurance company and lodged with the application for confirmation, once the separate petition has been made to the court for the appointment of the executor(s) dative. Such a bond of caution would not be required if there was a surviving spouse as the deceased's estate would pass to that spouse by the law of intestate succession in Scotland. (NB The premium for any required bond of caution depends on the values and circumstances of the estate.)

13. Pay any Inheritance Tax due at the time of application and arrange for instalment payments if any of the assets qualify. If you have completed Form IHT400 then that must be submitted and any tax due at the time of the application paid 20 working days before you can submit the probate application to the Probate Registry.

14. The Probate Registry or Sheriff Court sends the grant of probate or confirmation to you by post along with, in England and Wales, any additional probate copies (sealed copies) ordered or in Scotland, certificates of confirmation. (N.B. In Scotland, a certificate of confirmation relates to one specific item of estate.)

15. Send copies of the grant of probate or the appropriate certificate of confirmation to each organisation contacted in step 8 to show the executors' entitlement to deal with the deceased's assets. In return, organisations release the deceased's assets to the executors and close or transfer the deceased's accounts and files.

16. Advertise for creditors, if necessary. If any large or unexpected claims result, you should consider consulting a solicitor.

17. Respond to any queries raised by HMRC concerning the values of assets or liabilities of the estate. Agree final figures with them. Report any additional assets or liabilities that have come to light since probate or confirmation was granted.

18. When all assets are collected, pay debts, including any unpaid Income Tax and Capital Gains Tax relating to the deceased's income up to the time of death.

19. Ask HMRC for an Income Tax return or repayment claim form and complete it with details of the income of the estate to the end of the tax year during which the deceased died. Pay any tax due. A return may also be needed for each subsequent tax year if the administration of the estate isn't complete within one tax year.

20. Ask HMRC for Form IHT30 (Application for a Clearance Certificate) or download it from the gov.uk website; complete it and have it signed by all the executors and in due course receive the signed discharge certificate from HMRC.

21. Check that there have been no claims against the estate (in England or Wales under the Inheritance [Provision for Family and Dependants] Act 1975 during the six months following the grant of probate or confirmation and that there were no claims made by cohabitees in a Scottish estate in the six months after date of death. In Scotland, settle any claims for legal rights arising in testate cases; if legal rights are to be renounced by the entitled parties, obtain formal discharges, to be placed with the estate papers. Barring any such challenges, the estate can be distributed.

22. When all the assets have been accounted for and debts paid, legacies can be distributed. Get a receipt from each beneficiary.

23. Draw up estate accounts. Get approval of the accounts from all residuary beneficiaries (or those entitled under the intestacy laws) and send them copies. Make payment of final balance of residue due to beneficiaries. Issue HMRC Form R185 (Estate Income) to the residuary beneficiaries showing their shares of the income of the estate and the tax deducted from it during the tax year.

24. When all cheques have cleared, close the executors' account.

25. The administration of the estate is now complete. All accounts should be saved for 12 years, along with the other principal estate papers.

In Scotland, accounts should be saved for 20 years for legal rights, along with the other principal estate papers. Where there is a surviving spouse, copies of the paperwork should be kept for the purposes of administering the surviving spouse's estate and thereafter kept for 20 years after the death of the surviving spouse.